Book Selection and Collections:
A Comparison of German
and American University Libraries

Number Twelve
Columbia University Studies in Library Service

Book Selection and Collections:
A Comparison of German
and American University Libraries

by *J. Periam Danton*

COLUMBIA UNIVERSITY PRESS
New York and London

for Lois

who stoked the furnace

PREFACE

This study, undertaken in its most intensive aspects during a 1960–1961 sabbatical year in West Germany, is based in large part upon visits to its university libraries, talks and correspondence with their librarians, other officials, professors, and students, and on examination of documentary records. The existing pertinent secondary material has also been used. Similar investigation of American university libraries was for the most part done earlier.

There are at present eighteen universities in the Federal Republic of Germany. Of these, to the surprise of many, eight were founded or, like Cologne, Mainz, and Münster, were newly founded after long periods of quiescence, in this century. Four—the Free University of Berlin, Giessen, Mainz and Saarland—were begun or reestablished after World War II; two others—Hamburg and Cologne—after World War I. I had the privilege of visiting seventeen of the eighteen.

The study is concerned equally with the German and the American university library. The German reader may wish to skim over some of the historical and descriptive material in the first half of Chapters II and III; the American reader will already be familiar with much of what appears in the second half of those chapters. It is my hope that the discussion of basic philosophy and policy, especially in the Introduction and Chapters I, IV, V, and VI, will be of interest to university library personnel everywhere.

I have handled the somewhat troublesome matter of German words and quotations thus: Single words and short phrases are given in the text in literal translation with the original in parentheses immediately following. Quotations of any length have been either translated or summarized in the text with the original and the bibliographical source supplied in the notes. In quoting from older German literature I have retained the original spelling, as for example in such words as *Werth, Theil, bey, Cultur,* preferring faithfulness to the text to consistency with modern usage.

In order to save space and avoid repetition, in referring to both German and American institutions, I have omitted the words "university" and "library" except in cases where doing so would result in ambiguity; thus Bonn stands for University of Bonn (Library); Columbia, Columbia University (Library); Mainz, University of Mainz (Library); Stanford, Leland Stanford University (Library); etc.

I am greatly indebted to: the University of California for the sabbatical year's leave during which the major portion of the study was undertaken; the Department of State's International Educational Exchange Service for a Fulbright grant as Research Scholar; Messrs. Richard F. Timken-Zinkann and Franz Eschbach of the Fulbright Commission in Germany for helping to make my stay so pleasant; the Association of College and Research Libraries for a grant-in-aid; the Committee on Research of the University of California for clerical assistance; and my colleague, Professor Leroy C. Merritt, for allowing me the use of material gathered by him. To him, Professors Donald Coney, California, Wilhelm Martin Luther, Göttingen, and Stephen McCarthy, Cornell, I am indebted for many helpful suggestions resulting from their reading of a preliminary draft. Similar thanks are due Dean Jack Dalton, Dr. Richard Logsdon, and Dr. Maurice F. Tauber, of Columbia, who critically read the final draft. The study would not have been possible without the cooperation and help of university librarians on both sides of the Atlantic, and for their assistance I am most grateful.

It is a special pleasure to record my warm appreciation to the German librarians who devoted many hours of their time to me and displayed enormous friendliness and patience in responding to my often troublesome inquiries and requests. Nor can I fail to mention my indebtedness to the numerous staff members of German and American university libraries who provided me with the many kinds of information for which authors naturally turn to library personnel.

The debt is especially large to the staffs of the universities of California and Göttingen.

Dr. Gisela von Busse, of the *Deutsche Forschungsgemeinschaft,* Bad Godesberg, was kind enough to make available to me data which could not have been elsewhere secured. Her study, to which I have referred in Chapter III, is by far the best account in English of the present status and practices of West German scholarly libraries.

Mrs. Ian D. Currie, at one time Mrs. Liselotte Fajardo, Dr. Kenneth M. Glazier, and Miss Brenda Kuske, research assistants, University of California; Miss Renate Werner, University of Göttingen Library; and Mrs. Helen Simon, Berkeley, aided me greatly in bibliographical and reference work. The maps were especially drawn for the study by Mr. Stephen Gildersleeve, Berkeley. To Mrs. George Maltese, Mrs. Ruby Massen, and Mrs. Hedwig Doehring, I owe much thanks for typing drafts of the manuscript and other clerical labors.

Finally, I tender particular thanks to Wilhelm Martin Luther, director (1958–1962) of the Niedersächsische Staats- und Universitätsbibliothek, Göttingen, where, at his invitation, I made my headquarters and where I was accorded every conceivable facility, privilege, and courtesy. The best testimony I can offer to the friendliness and helpfulness of Dr. Luther and the members of his staff is that I very shortly came to feel as much *"zu Haus"* in their Library as I do in that of my own university. It seems fitting that I record my sense of great personal bereavement, and of the loss to scholarly librarianship everywhere, resulting from Doctor Luther's tragic death on June 2, 1962.

J. PERIAM DANTON

Berkeley
September, 1962

CONTENTS

TABLES

MAPS AND FIGURE

INTRODUCTION

This study is concerned with the selection of books and the development of book collections for university libraries in the Federal Republic of Germany and the United States. The concern is particularly with the philosophy and policy of book selection. The word "selection" is used in its exact sense to mean the choice of materials. Activities such as order and purchase, performed only after selection decisions have been made, are not embraced. The word "policy," on the other hand, is used in a broad sense to mean the fundamental issues underlying the selection program. Such matters as value judgments and the bibliographical sources for the selection of individual titles are, therefore, excluded.

The critical importance of the role of book selection may be demonstrated in several ways. Two points may be made at the outset. The "best" selection would ideally bring to the library the largest number of items useful to the teaching and research programs of the parent institution and no items not useful to them. As we move away from this theoretical ideal there is (a) an indeterminate number of needed titles which are not acquired and (b) an indeterminate number of titles that are acquired but are not currently and *may* never be needed. Under (a), the program of teaching and research suffers. Under (b), money is wastefully expended for selection, acquisition, cataloging, shelving, and maintenance in perpetuity. Total costs, including processing and housing, for purchased and for gift or exchange items in a large American university library have been computed as at least ten dollars and six dollars a volume respectively; in the German library, where salary scales and construction costs are lower, perhaps half of these amounts.[1] Educational and economic considerations both clearly point to the need for the highest possible quality of selection. University librarians on both sides of the Atlantic are in agreement on this point as well as on the difficulty of the problem of insuring the desired results. Book selection is, indeed, in consequence, "the foremost scholarly business of the library." [2]

"I venture to say that (a) the most important, and (b) one of the most difficult activities in . . . a [large, university, research] library is the selection of books and other materials." [3] Almost precisely the same thought is expressed by a colleague: "The greatest single problem in acquisition for a research library . . . is the selection of the new books . . . to be bought and the rejection of those that will not be needed." [4] Elsewhere the same writer lists, in first place, among the six "great library problems," the question, "What should be the book selection policy of a large library?" [5] The same conviction is stated by a German librarian: "The most important task of the librarian is to see that the right books are bought at the right time. The fine and difficult office of the librarian is to select and weigh— to decide with feeling for quality and relationships—from the huge abundance." [6]

The simple truth should not be forgotten, that a title cannot be purchased, added by gift or exchange, cataloged, classified, borrowed, or used until someone has made a selection-decision.

It is therefore here assumed that the selection of books is a matter of prime importance to university libraries because the development of library collections is controlled by it, and because the quality of the collection is one of the two major factors that determines whether the library supports well or poorly the teaching and research programs of the institution of which it is a part. It is further assumed that an examination of the basic issues that make up selection policy and the essential elements of its implementation may be of value in shedding light on the complex and urgent problems confronting all university libraries in their efforts to serve adequately the research and teaching needs of their institutions.

The basic issues of book selection policy, to which all other aspects and practices may be subsumed, may be briefly described as follows:

1. The relation of book selection and the collections which result
   from it to the function of the university. This issue involves a
   determination of the institutional program, policy, and teaching and research level in the various fields of learning.
2. The location of responsibility, particularly the ultimate responsibility, for selection and for the expenditure of book funds.
3. The performance of actual selection, whether by members of
   the library staff, by members of the faculty, or by a combination of the two.
4. The means by which selection is carried on.
5. The nature of the materials to be collected and the levels of
   collecting.

A university library is defined as a library attached to an institution of higher learning, a major function of which is research and
the advancement of knowledge in a wide variety of subjects and
which, in these subjects, offers the doctor's degree. As a minimum,
this means the principal disciplines of the humanities and the social,
biological, physical, and earth sciences.

A dominant, indeed, perhaps *the* dominant characteristic of university libraries is that they are "open-ended" collections; a finite
limit cannot, at least in any foreseeable future, be placed upon their
ultimate size. This is so because the world of knowledge is constantly expanding, proliferating, fractionating. Hence printed matter in new fields is regularly published—to say nothing, of course,
of revisions, modifications, and reassessments of older literature, or
of the present availability of such literature not now owned by a
library but of interest to it. Nothing that the history of the printed
book since the fifteenth century has taught us suggests that the volume of print and near-print matter is likely to decrease in the future.
All the evidence we have points, in fact, to the opposite conclusion.

The libraries are "open-ended," also, because, except in limited
and quite insignificant ways, they cannot weed, discard or elimi-
nate. Thus, though a Midwest Inter-Library Center or an interinstitutional specialized collecting agreement may slow the rate of
growth of a library, and though microreproduction or compact storage will reduce the rate of spatial growth, growth in absolute terms,

however slow, is bound to occur.[7] World War II visited catastrophe upon many German libraries, reducing their collections by a quarter, a half, or even more. Münster lost sixty-six percent of its total holdings; [8] Hamburg's loss, 710,000 of 870,000 volumes, was over 80 percent.[9] Disaster of this kind constitutes a very special case which, however, does not invalidate our point. All but three libraries had, in fact, by 1960, surpassed their prewar sizes; in a decade or less, the three will also have done so.

Further, as knowledge increases, as new fields and subfields develop, universities, by the very nature of their obligations to society, absorb them into their programs of teaching and research. "It is reasonable to suppose, therefore, that the University Library will continue to grow steadily unless it is stopped by administrative fiat, complacency, or calamity," wrote Metcalf in his last report as Director at Harvard.[10] This axiom applies to any university library.

A second characteristic of university libraries is that they are nearly "universal" collections.[11] They must, that is, select from virtually the entire world output of literature, which is now estimated at more than 240,000 titles annually,[12] plus the scores of thousands of items offered each year by the second-hand market.

The number of items of print—quite aside from manuscript and nearprint—which have appeared since Gutenberg is unknown. Iwinski, in his well-known study, calculated a world production of about 10,400,000 book and 71,248 journal titles by 1908.[13] No equally thorough international study gives an up-to-date estimate, but it would be conservative to say that the figures today are at least double those of 1908.[14] Nearly 120,000 titles appear in the 1943 edition of the *Union List of Serials* with additional thousands in its two *Supplements* and a *Southeastern Supplement*.[15]

The near-universality of the library of the kind under consideration is exemplified by such statements as these: "A genuinely outstanding work on any subject at all is likely to be of interest to scholars in areas other than its own, so it would be difficult to name any topic on which a library like Harvard's would never buy a book." [16] "Only technology, veterinary medicine, and agriculture (excluding viticulture) are, in general, given no consideration." [17] "The Library acquires the literature of scholarly importance of all fields." [18] The "open-endedness," the near universality, and the function of conservation make the university library, truly, as Schopenhauer said less accurately of libraries generally, "the only sure and continuing memory of mankind." [19]

The study assumes that the era when even the wealthiest library in the world could reasonably expect to acquire everything in print ended sometime in the nineteenth century. (The nineteenth century librarian might not have agreed.) From this assumption stems a second; namely, that every library is somehow and to some degree engaged in selection. In fact, it may be argued, and is here argued, that book selection is not only a fundamental and abiding aspect of the operation of libraries, but also one of the two basic factors that determines library excellence.

The large university libraries, like the major national libraries are, therefore, the closest approximation the twentieth century can show to the "universal library" concept of an earlier day, by which was meant the ideal of bibliographic completeness. This concept can be traced back at least as far as the sixteenth century to Conrad Gesner's *Bibliotheca Universalis* of 1545–1555. The concept, a chimeric human vision of the perfect, was avowedly pursued by Gottlieb Georgi in the eighteenth century, by Jacques Brunet and Johann Grässe in the nineteenth, and by the Brussels Union Catalog of the International Institute of Bibliography in the twentieth. In libraries, also, the idea persisted for centuries and, indeed, was in some quarters not formally abandoned until recent years. Anthony Panizzi held it for the British Museum in the middle of the nineteenth century. The philosophy, at least, of building a universal library, existed at Erlangen until World War I and even, to some extent, to World War II.[20] "The ideal objective of [a great research library] is a complete record of human thought, emotion, and action. Its collections should be developed without distinction as to language, date, place, and form of publication. In short, it should have everything." [21]

The practical possibility of the ideal of bibliographic completeness is no longer anywhere responsibly maintained. But, as has been suggested, university libraries are the nearest heir of this ideal and, in the sense that they acquire and preserve materials from the entire

world of learning, they come close to the idea of "universal." As
such, as the memory of mankind, as the bridges from past to future,
and as the chief means—not even excepting national libraries—
through which discovery will be made and learning advanced, their
importance to our civilization cannot be overemphasized.

The decision to undertake a comparative study of German and
American university libraries was the result of several considerations: (1) It was in Germany that the idea of the "modern" university library first took root with the founding of the University of
Göttingen in 1737. The Göttingen library was the prototype of the
present-day European research library and strongly influenced other
university libraries not only throughout Germany but also on most
of the European continent, including Scandinavia. The founding of
the real university in America, beginning with the Johns Hopkins
University in 1876, in many respects followed the German pattern.
(2) Certain American university library practices and phenomena,
such as the concepts of "universality" and "comprehensiveness," the
faculty library committee, and the specialized seminar or departmental collection, were derived from German example.[22] The
German-trained or influenced founders and first professors at Johns
Hopkins were so imbued with the idea of the seminar library that
the University was begun without any central library whatever.
Shortly after its 1892 founding there were more volumes in the numerous departmental libraries of the University of Chicago than
there were in the central library, if one omits the large Berlin purchase.[23] (3) Book selection for university libraries in Germany, in
recent years, has followed a path quite different from that in the
United States, with reduction to nearly zero of the role of the faculty
and expansion to virtually one hundred percent of the role of the
library staff. (4) The development of major university libraries
during this century has been more marked in the United States than
anywhere else.

In West Germany today there are eighteen universities (or seventeen if one omits Giessen which, since its rebirth in 1950, has not
yet developed the full complement of faculties). The eighteen are
listed below in alphabetical order. Except for the University of Saarland at Saarbrücken, the name of the university is in each case the

same as the name of the city of its location. The dates of establishment and re-establishment are given in parentheses.

Berlin (Free University) (1948)	Heidelberg (1386)
Bonn (1786; 1818)	Kiel (1665)
Cologne ᵃ (Köln) (1388; 1919)	Mainz (1476; 1946)
Erlangen (1743)	Marburg (1527)
Frankfurt ᵃ (1914)	Munich (München) (1472; 1826)
Freiburg (1457)	Münster (1780; 1880; 1902)
Giessen (1607; 1950)	Saarland (1947)
Göttingen ᵃ (1737)	Tübingen (1477)
Hamburg ᵃ (1919)	Würzburg (1582)

ᵃ A state and university library (*Staats- und Universitätsbibliothek*) or city and university library (*Stadt- und Universitätsbibliothek*).

In the United States the number is much less readily determined. It is certainly close to fifty; it may be as large as seventy-five; it is possibly upward of one hundred. The precise number of the group is of no importance but its nature is. In this connection it is useful to note that, in the eleven-year period, 1948–1958, about 85 percent of all doctors' degrees granted in the United States were awarded by the "top" fifty universities; forty institutions were responsible for 80 percent of the degrees.[24] These include (1) the seven pre-Revolutionary private colleges, which are now universities, of the New England and Middle Atlantic States, and the more recently founded private institutions like Chicago, Cornell, Duke, Johns Hopkins, Northwestern, Rochester, and Stanford, and (2) the major state universities, almost all established in the nineteenth century.

The student who examines the existing bibliographies will find several hundred titles of books and articles devoted in whole or in part to the subject of book selection and acquisition. It is a remarkable fact, however, that relatively little of this writing is concerned with the university library and that still less is devoted to a consideration of the basic issues of selection policy. Remarkable, since university libraries as a group are among the largest and most expensive of all libraries, are beset to at least as great a degree as any others with problems of demand versus available funds, and have twin, often conflicting, obligations to the present and to the future.

The point may be underlined by recalling some of the more extensive treatments of the subject: Asheim's *Humanities and the Li-*

brary (1957); Carter and Bonk's *Building Library Collections* (1959); Danton's *The Climate of Book Selection* (1959); Drury's *Book Selection* (1930); Haines's *Living with Books: The Art of Book Selection* (1950); Peñalosa's *La Selección y Adquisición de Libros* (1961); Pennsylvania University Library's *Changing Patterns of Scholarship and the Future of Research Libraries* (1951); Ranganathan's *Library Book Selection* (1952); Tauber's *Technical Services in Libraries* (1954); Wellard's *Book Selection* (1937); and Wilson's *The Practice of Book Selection* (1940). Similar and more extensive citations of the journal literature could be made.

The foregoing is not, of course, in any sense intended as a criticism of the various authors for not doing what they did not set out to do, but simply underscores the fact that few have interested themselves—in print—with the philosophical questions involved in the selection of books for university libraries. Redenbacher, in the first note to an extensive study says: "The English and American literature on book selection applies almost exclusively to public libraries and need not here be taken into consideration." [25] As Redenbacher's later citations of Anglo-American writing tacitly acknowledge, the judgment is a little harsh.

The nonmonographic literature, chiefly in journals, contains a number of pertinent titles. The study which throws most light on the subject and one, incidentally, which does not appear in the standard bibliographies, is Redenbacher's just cited "Acquisition" (*"Die Erwerbung"*), especially the second part, "Principles and Methods of Selection" (*"Grundsätze und Methoden der Auswahl"*).[26] However, much even of this comprehensive, objectively comparative, and excellently documented study is concerned with such questions as problems and techniques of acquisition, budgets and costs, bibliographical aids, reviews, and censorship. Among additional treatments which are variously useful are a number by Bauhuis, Bishop, Downs, Fussler, Hamilton, Leyh, Metcalf, Swank, and Tiemann. As these and some others are referred to in later chapters, bibliographical data are not given here.

A review of the literature of the subject must also take account of the few existing statements of selection policy. Redenbacher and others have observed the remarkable paucity of such statements and have suggested or implied their desirability.[27] "I undertook to ask about fifteen university librarians how they managed the work of book selection, and if they had a written statement (detailed or otherwise) of acquisition policy. The answer to the first question uniformly was 'badly'. The answer to the second, in each case was 'no'. You are digging into the sore area of university library management." [28] Since these lines were written, several university libraries have put their policies into near-print statements, although in some cases the documents are more concerned with the acquisition of materials than the *who, what,* and *why* of selecting them. In 1960 Branscomb elicited from the members of the Association of Research Libraries information on acquisition policy statements. There were, at the time, forty-two university-members of the Association. Of these, thirty-seven responded to Branscomb's questionnaire. Four of these reported that they had "full" policy statements. Eight others reported the existence of "partial" statements, and four indicated that they were in the process of writing statements. A majority of those responding believed that it was both possible and valuable to formulate a written policy.[29]

Among the more comprehensive and pertinent statements now in existence are those of Cornell, Harvard, Illinois, Louisiana State, Michigan, Oregon State, Pennsylvania, Purdue, Southern Illinois, and the University of Oregon. As these are referred to in the succeeding chapters, especially Chapter III, bibliographical citations are not given here. It is clear, of course, that every library operates on the basis of a policy, good, bad, or indifferent, expressed or implied, or only practically sensed through tradition and usage.[30] It is also unfortunately, and perhaps inevitably true, however, that, where written and explicit policy is lacking, library staff and faculty are frequently not clear as to just what the library's policies are.[31]

One other aspect of the literature deserves mention. The German university in general, and the German university library in particular, are blessed with a very large body of solid historical, factual, and critical studies. There is at least one and there are usually several for each of the universities as well as for each of the university libraries. One not untypical example may be cited for illustration. Max Buchner's *Aus der Vergangenheit der Universität Würzburg*

(Berlin, Springer, 1932) is a large octavo of 799 pages. The contribution on the library contains a five and a half page bibliography, more than fifty items of which *specifically* concern the library. Most of the material, even in the library histories, is not directly relevant to the present study. There is, nonetheless, a good deal of pertinent information in them on book-collecting policy and development of collections.

No one, certainly, can accuse the German academician of having neglected the study of his own institution or its library. The same, unfortunately, cannot be said of the United States; though we have several times as many universities, one would have difficulty pointing to more than a score of sound historical studies, and the number of such works on individual university libraries is even fewer.

CHAPTER I

The University, the Library, Book Selection, and Book Collections

Book selection and collection building can be considered only in terms of the tasks and obligations of the library and they, in turn, derive or should derive from the functions of the university. As to these, there appears to be virtual unanimity and little room for argument: the primary functions of the university are teaching, the interpretation and conservation of knowledge, and the search for truth, or research. Documentation or evidence on this axiom, or on the basic tasks of the library, seems unnecessary. On two aspects of its function, however, quotation of the comment of one scholar, former president, and teacher may be permitted:

the university library, more than any other institution whatsoever, is the custodian of the world's actual knowledge and the reservoir of its potential knowledge. More than any other institution it preserves and makes available the results of previous human seeking; more than any other institution it makes possible the fruitful continuation of that search. That is a strong statement, but I am confident that it is sound. For the university library certainly performs this double function more fully than any institution that is not a library, and more fully, in this country at least, than any other type of library, public or private. Many libraries of other types share significantly in the ministry of learning, but the scholarly purpose, in such libraries, is either not dominant or, if dominant, is limited in its range. The Library of Congress is a unique and worthy companion of the university library in this respect; but the scholarly primacy of the university library as a type is clear.[1]

The major obligation of the university library, with respect to its book selection and book collections, is to provide the materials which will now and in the future best contribute to the fulfillment of these closely related functions of teaching, conservation, and research. For reasons already noted—the overwhelming volume of print, the impossibility of any library acquiring everything, the inability accurately to predict "in the future" needs, among others— the statement is, as every university librarian knows, deceptively simple.

In a real even though figurative sense, the many fields of learning, none wholly isolated from all others, are bound together in a great fabric of knowledge, warp and woof touching at innumerable points. These points of mutual contact constantly change, increase and decrease, the cloth ceaselessly lengthens and broadens. The library is the university's sole instrument capable of reflecting the entire panorama of this tapestry. The library is also, consequently, the university's sole instrument capable of reflecting the totality of the institution's major purposes, and of the relationships and interdependencies of its many departments and faculties. It does so through its provision of a university-wide spectrum of graphic materials and, notably, of the important works which cut across two or more fields, the works of synthesis, of general cultural history, of the development of the different disciplines. The library is usually the major "laboratory" and research instrument of the university, and it is the only one indispensable to all its departments. It is thus not simply an image of the university but it is the only true image of the totality of that for which the university stands and exists. Many have expressed the thought, which can be neither too strongly emphasized, nor for a moment ignored, "that the library is the one central, all-important institution making possible or impossible by its strength or its weakness real university work by students and instructors alike." [2] If, as Lord Haldane said, "it is in the Universities . . . that we see how the soul of a people . . . mirrors itself," we may claim with at least equal assurance that it is in its library that the soul of a university mirrors itself.[3] From this functional and representational universality, the library derives its fundamental imperative of book selection and collection building.

Teaching and research are, at least beyond the American undergraduate level, and perhaps beyond the lower division level, indivisible. Nonetheless, we can distinguish, at least in general terms, between two very broad classes of library materials: those which

KÖNIGSBERG →
(U.S.S.R. ✷)

BRAUNSBERG →
(POLAND ▲)

KIEL ●

✷ROSTOCK ✷GREIFSWALD

HAMBURG ●

⊞ Bremen

WEST GERMANY

▲ OSNABRÜCK

BERLIN ● ✷ BERLIN

FRANKFURT
a-ODER ▲

▲ RINTELN

● MÜNSTER

✖ HELMSTEDT

EAST GERMANY

▲ PADERBORN

▲ WITTENBERG

BRESLAU
(POLAND✷)
→

⊞ Bochum
▲ DUISBURG

GÖTTINGEN ●

✷ HALLE

KASSEL ▲

✷ LEIPZIG

● COLOGNE

ERFURT ▲ ✷ JENA

● BONN

● MARBURG

▲ HERBORN

● GIESSEN

FULDA ▲

● FRANKFURT a-MAIN

0 15 30 45 60 75 90 105

▲ TRIER

● MAINZ

▲ BAMBERG

MILES

● WÜRZBURG

0   30   60   90   120 150 180

SAARLAND
●

● HEIDELBERG

● ERLANGEN

KILOMETERS

▲ ALTDORF

BRÜNN
OLMÜTZ
(CZECH. ▲)

STRASSBURG ✷

▲ STUTTGART

⊞ Regensburg

▲ INGOLSTADT

● TÜBINGEN

▲ DILLINGEN

● FREIBURG

● MUNICH

GERMAN UNIVERSITIES, PAST AND PRESENT

●   West German Universities

✷   Universities in East Germany
    or otherwise lost to West Germany

▲   Universities abolished, 1798–1818

⊞   Universities being established

extend the frontiers of knowledge and constitute contributions to it, or which enable the scholar to make such a contribution, and those which do not. In the latter group fall most texts, syntheses, introductory works, and many historical treatments and biographies; in short, what we may loosely call "secondary" or "teaching" materials.[4]

In the first class belong the monographs and research studies which tell us something new, the source materials such as manuscripts, many early journals, and documents.[5] This does not, obviously, mean that an item in the "teaching" class may not upon occasion be of value to the scholar. The elementary Japanese grammar and glossary are not of any value to the Japanolog, but to the literary historian studying Lafcadio Hearn, it may be an essential tool for understanding the writing of that expatriate. Nor does the distinction mean, as is often also the case, that research studies are not used in teaching, even at lower levels. "It is increasingly difficult to identify any of the Library's resources as exclusively useful for research and valueless to the teaching program." [6] The line between the two classes is often functionally very blurred. It means, simply, that some kinds of print are more useful for general instructional purposes than for research, and vice versa.

For "teaching," up to a fairly advanced academic level, the student does not need, and cannot use, the 1906 report of the Bulgarian national railways, the Argentinian government edict of 1882, a research study in Chinese of the poetry of Li Tai Po, a research study in Dutch on the painting of Memling, a monograph in German on the holographic comments on a Goethe manuscript, or a treatise in English on Sir Robert Bruce Cotton's *A Short View of the Long Life and Raigne of Henry the Third*. Only the scholar or the student as would-be scholar needs and can use items such as these.

From almost every point of view—selection, acquisition, cataloging, and classification—but especially from the point of view of selection, it is the research class of material which causes the library its greatest problems, doubts, and questions. The reasons are several. Such materials are published in many languages; there is almost no limit, even in a sub-subdivision of a field of learning, to the number of separate titles available; they are often costly to learn about (let alone to acquire, catalog, and house); and, above all, it is extraordinarily difficult to determine what the scholar will most need, not only now but in the future. By contrast, for the student in any given subject we need provide a relatively limited number of works only, chiefly in his native language, mostly contemporary or nearly so, and we need not be greatly concerned if the few hundred, or possibly thousand titles his grandson will need are quite different. But the value of the library as a research instrument lies in its relative completeness in the fields of interest to the university's scholars, and the materials used by a professor today may also be used, though possibly in different ways, and for different purposes, by his successor fifty years hence. The contemporary record of prices of representative consumers' goods and services enables the economist to say what income the citizen requires in order to maintain a certain standard of living. The same record, at a future date, may be used by a political scientist to trace the effect of a steadily increasing cost of living on voter behavior.

To "teach" the subject of Victorian poetry, or nineteenth century German dramatic literature, we need only a score or so of good histories, an equal number of reference works—useful for other subjects as well—and standard biographies, editions, and anthologies of about the same number of poets and dramatists. But to provide a significant research library for the scholar or the doctoral student in the two fields, we need a body of material that comes perilously close to infinity in its compass and includes drafts, manuscripts, letters, diaries, first editions, translations, commentaries, and definitive editions, not only of these poets and dramatists, but also of those who influenced them or may have done so, and those whom they influenced or may have influenced, as well as extensive material on the social and cultural history of their times and so on and so on.

The quality, that is the value for research, of a university library ten or fifty or a hundred years from now is a direct result of its day-to-day selection and acquisition in the intervening years, just as its value today is the direct result of this activity during the previous years of its history. Put another way, we may say that, whereas even today, given sufficient funds, a very good library for a school, *gymnasium,* or college can be created in a few years or a decade, it is not possible in the twentieth century, no matter what the available means, to build a significant research library in short order. It took forty years of devoted effort in the acquisition of materials, as well as millions of dollars, to bring the Library of the University of California at Los Angeles to its 1960 stature—thirteenth in size among American university libraries. The libraries of the Free University of Berlin, founded in 1948, and Mainz, newly founded in 1946, had in 1960 holdings of only about 380,000 volumes. Thousands of volumes that these libraries, and many other much older ones, want and should have are difficult and expensive to acquire, or are out of print and simply not available for purchase in their original format.

So the major problem in book selection and collection building concerns research materials, both those currently published and the large mass constantly being offered by the second-hand book market. Ideally, perhaps, in order to provide all material when need arises, the university library should acquire, at the time of publication or other contemporary availability, every item that will ever be needed by any of those whom it is to serve. (This assumes that some material, if not acquired contemporaneously, will not be available when future need occurs.) A library founded in 1440 which had done so, and had not since suffered loss, would possess an ideal research collection so far as printed materials are concerned. Its holdings might total something like thirty million bound volumes and another thirty or forty million manuscripts, maps, pamphlets, broadsides, etc. Hundreds of thousands of items, new and second-hand, are now available each year. In a practical world, the factor of cost alone requires that a selection be made from what is available at any time. The selection, of course, should be done in such a way as to satisfy the largest number of present and future research needs. The contention, sometimes made, that the satisfaction of future needs is more difficult than the satisfaction of present ones is partly illusory. To be sure, the need of today's scholar can be, and is, made known by him, if what he requires is not now available in his library; whereas, the need of tomorrow's scholar is not known, and cannot be certainly known until he appears. But the scholar today who requires a publication of the 1920s which is not in his library has presumably no better chance of having his need

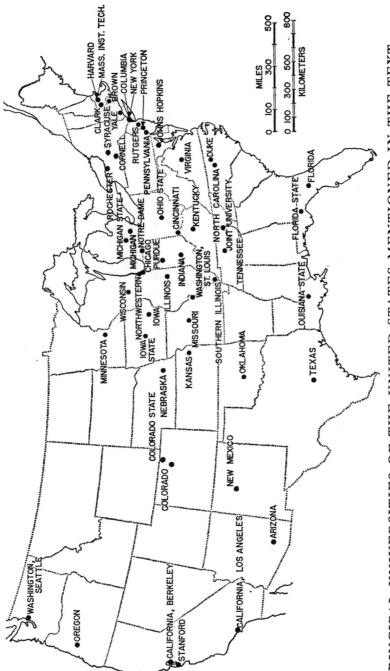

PRINCIPAL UNIVERSITIES OF THE UNITED STATES MENTIONED IN THE TEXT

fulfilled than the scholar of 2000 will have of finding a work, not in
his library then, which was published in the 1960s.

The problem is not simply of the need fifty or even ten years
hence but rather of *all* future need, that is, all need not specifically
known today. The library cannot in any degree avoid the obligation
of collecting and conserving what it deems to be of most value for
the present, for next semester, next year, and the distant future.

But these needs, created by the chance idea that comes to a man,
by the footnote reference he happens to read, by the question of a
student, by conversation with a colleague, by an investigation already pursued or in progress, and in numbers of other ways, as well
as by the direction which research fifty or twenty or ten or five years
hence will take are frequently—perhaps one should say usually—
not predictable. They are certainly not definitely predictable. To be
sure, we all know that scholars will probably never cease being interested in Bismarck, Lincoln, the Renaissance, the Reformation—
the great men and events of the past. This is hindsight and easy. It
was even easy to know, at the outset of World War II, that materials
on that catastrophe would interest the historian as long as the civilization it saved lasts. But what university librarian was wise enough
to begin collecting the first items on the origins of Nazism in Munich
in the early 1920s? Who in the 1860s collected the diaries of Civil
War soldiers? How many university libraries in 1896 acquired Edwin Arlington Robinson's *The Torrent and the Night Before*, or
seventy years earlier, Heine's *Gedichte?* Thousands of other similar
questions could be asked to which the same negative answer would
have to be given. The fact, of course, is that every university library
is constantly buying at high prices material, including much from
its own geographical back yard, which could have been had almost
for the asking when it first appeared. As these lines were written,
the University of Göttingen Library paid at auction about $2,300 for
a very small diary covering one year in the life of Georg Christoph
Lichtenberg (1742–1799), German satirist and physicist, who was a
professor at the University during the last quarter century of his life.
At about the same time dozens of other university libraries were
making similar purchases at comparable prices.

If the history of university library collections and their use teaches us anything, it is that libraries have been too passive, too conservative in their collection building and have paid too little attention to the potentially but not obviously useful and important material around them. "Selection of books for a library like this calls for an attempt to foresee the future course of research and to obtain publications that, though they seem insignificant today, will be wanted by scholars tomorrow." [7] The fact that most major university libraries in this century have grown out of proportion to the increase in the publication rate and have found it desirable to increase the scope of their collecting, is at least partial evidence. The University of California, to cite just one of a score of examples which might be adduced had, as recently as 1946, a collection of 1,300,000 volumes and collected little or nothing from certain areas such as India and Africa; in 1960 it had a collection of 2,500,000 volumes and "the area aspect of collecting has been broadened until it is virtually global." [8] Materials on "India, South Africa, Latin America, Franciscans, Egypt, Semitic Languages," areas neglected before 1947, are now collected by Cornell.[9]

The thesis is sometimes advanced that: (1) as the future is obscure and bound to bring change it will therefore (2) reveal needs which we cannot today know; consequently, (3) we cannot plan for the university library's future. The major and minor premises are unarguable. But to accept the conclusion is to abdicate from the use of reason; to deny, that is, the application of the intellect in making rational even if not always wholly accurate predictions from knowledge of past and present fact.

The university, as a part of the society in which it exists, does not function in a vacuum. It is influenced by social change of many kinds and especially by the development of knowledge. It is also influenced by the relative importance to society, or which society attaches to, the fields of knowledge at any time. The status of the fields of learning will no doubt be different a hundred or fifty and possibly even ten years hence than it is today. To take a very broad and prime example we need think only of the relative positions in society and in the university of theology and physics one hundred years ago and now. Much of this kind of development is unforeseen and unforeseeable. Consequently, the university cannot be expected to tell the library, or anyone else: Here is our program, here are the fields we cover and to what extent, now and forever more. The library, however, should attempt to secure such a program statement covering at least a five year period. This kind of university teaching and research program statement, elicited by the library and its faculty advisors, seems essential to anything like long-range library selection and collection policy. But such a statement, indispensable though it is, is only long-range, not permanent. It may be added that statements of this kind are not conspicuous phenomena in universities.

At this point we may underscore the effect and significance of a fact unhappily too well-known to most university librarians. This is the not uncommon practice of universities to inaugurate programs of instruction and research without providing the library with adequate notice and, indeed, frequently without giving any advance thought to the library implications of the programs. The opposite side of the coin, the abandonment of an existing program, though of less frequent occurrence, is also noteworthy. As much probably as the riding of their hobbies by individual faculty members or the failure of librarians to maintain program-related balance in their collections, it has been responsible for the existence in our libraries of large and expensive groups of books which are now of relatively little interest to any one in the institution. The foregoing views appear to have virtually universal support. Fussler has noted, "we are forced to recognize that great research strength cannot usually be established in a library quickly. . . . Conversely . . . great research strength . . . once established, has an institutional kind of survival that is greater than the . . . institutional lifetime of the scholars and librarians . . . who contributed to the establishment of the strength." [10]

It should be obvious that if a university is to begin a program in African studies or embark for the first time on doctoral work in microbiology or Scandinavian literature, the library should not only be informed well ahead of time, but it might also appropriately be consulted as to probable long-range financial requirements and other pertinent considerations. Too frequently the library is suddenly faced with a *fait accompli* and with a group of eager teachers and researchers who assume that their library needs will at once be met. The common result is that the regular library collecting program is disrupted, sometimes for several years, and that existing plans for library growth and development have to be seriously and hastily revised. And of course, the library needs in the new field cannot be well met "at once." This is not simply a librarians' complaint but a matter having the gravest educational and financial implications for the university as a whole. Happily it is beginning to be recognized as such outside library walls. A Columbia committee took cognizance of "several striking instances of recent failure . . . to recognize and provide for library costs involved in new projects adopted by the University and [the library authorities] give several illustrations of the puzzling character of the issues they are called upon to consider and decide without, they feel, adequate information regarding . . . university policy." [11]

As the University of Illinois has formally and succinctly put both sides of the coin: "If we were to discontinue buying in a field in which we are now strong, there would be a rapid deterioration in the value of our present holdings. If we were to decide to start building up a previously neglected area we would find that great research strength cannot be established quickly or at small cost." [12]

In view of the preceding discussion, it seems essential to sound selecting and collecting policy, "That every library secure from the administrators of its institution a clear statement of institutional aims and objectives and that development . . . of the library be integrated and coordinated with these objectives as completely as possible." [13] One would add after the word "administrators" the phrase "and faculty," and note that it is not simply a "statement of institutional aims and objectives," but also a declaration of teaching and research program level that is required.

CHAPTER II

Early Collecting and Collections

The word "early" refers to the period up to the last quarter of the nineteenth century. The chronological division, like most such which have to do with institutional history, is somewhat arbitrary. It may seem questionable to put into a single early period a discussion of German libraries many of which, by 1875, had had a history of two hundred to nearly five hundred years. The justification for doing so will, it is hoped, be made clear in the following pages. Suffice it to say here that as late as the mid-nineteenth century not more than five German university libraries, and none in America, had really significant collections, and that the great growth and development, in Germany as well as in America, did not take place until after 1875.[1] Note will be taken of exceptions, and we need to bear in mind that from the latter part of the eighteenth century until the end of the nineteenth, the development in Germany—in terms of fiscal support, use, and in other ways—was about fifty to seventy-five years ahead of that in America.

Beginning around 1800, the German university won for itself an enormous, justly earned reputation, and for the next hundred years was generally held to be without peer.[2] By 1792, forty-two universities—more than in any other country—had been established on the territory of the future German *Reich*, though half of these institutions were abolished by 1818. It is of passing interest to find that four of the many Americans, and three of the first who came to Germany—Göttingen it was—to study made a lasting impress on American libraries: Joseph Green Cogswell, (1816–1818), who after unsuccessfully attempting to put his Göttingen-derived ideas into effect as librarian at Harvard, (1820–1823), went on to create the great Astor Library; Edward Everett, (1815–1817), a founder of the Boston Public Library; John Pierpont Morgan, (1854–1856), with the Morgan Library; and George Ticknor, (1815–1817), a founder and lavish benefactor of the Boston Public Library.

As a consequence of the reputation of the German universities, we may be blinded to the fact that, with the single exception of Göttingen, the libraries of these institutions were, until well into the nineteenth century, very feeble instruments indeed.[3] One may go somewhat further than this and say that, aside from Göttingen, the determining foundations of the libraries did not begin to be laid much before the end of the first quarter of the nineteenth century when regular state budgets were first granted.[4] At a comparable period in their history, that is, up to nearly the end of the nineteenth century, most American university libraries were also very feeble instruments. The reasons in each country were approximately the same. Regular book budgets were tiny or nonexistent; the collections were almost exclusively the result of more or less chance gifts; teaching was by textbook; and, in Germany, the relatively little real graduate work and faculty research were accomplished mainly by means of the large private library of the professor. Proof positive exists, in fact, that the personal collections of numerous professors were as large as, or larger than, the entire university library. The universities in both countries had the kind of libraries they needed at the time. The fact that little was "needed" for the educational programs of the institutions is amply demonstrated, on both sides of the Atlantic, by the very scanty hours of opening of the libraries and the severe restrictions on their use.

Thus, toward the end of the eighteenth century Bonn (1795) had about 15,000 volumes; Freiburg (1784), 30,000; Heidelberg (1795), 12,000; Kiel (1785), 30,000; Mainz (1785), 8,000; Münster (1784), 10,000; and Würzburg (1802), 16,000. Universities no longer in existence or now in East Germany were no better off. Breslau (1811) had 8,000–9,000; Frankfurt-an-der-Oder (1775), 25,000; Greifswald (1771), 20,000; Halle (1780), 12,000; Ingolstadt (1786), 40,000; and Leipzig (1789), 20,000 volumes.[5] Freiburg, Halle, Heidelberg, Kiel, Leipzig, and Würzburg were between one hundred fifty and four hundred years old.

At this time, of course, none of the American institutions of higher education was a university and none had a library of over a few

thousand volumes. Shores, on the basis of an extensive examination
of source and other materials, noted that "the major portion of
colonial college library holdings resulted from direct or indirect
benefactions" and that "the proportion of accessions acquired by direct purchase was probably less than a tenth of the total." [6] This
general situation continued well into the nineteenth century and in
many institutions up to and even beyond the mid-century years.
Harvard, then as now the largest academic library, had, in 1790,
12,000 volumes, "almost entirely the fruit of individual munificence,"
which was still the case by 1830.[7] Harvard's library of around 5,000
volumes was almost totally destroyed by fire in 1764.

The purpose of this brief note is not in any sense to belittle the
value of donations, many of which must be counted as the chief
treasures and crown jewels of university libraries both in Germany
and the United States, but rather to point out that, up to the beginning of the nineteenth century, we cannot speak of book selection, much less of book-selection policy, for the university libraries
of either country—Göttingen being the sole exception.

In striking contrast to its sister institutions, Göttingen, at the turn
of the century, could count the remarkable total of nearly 200,000
volumes. It stood head and shoulders not only above all the other
German university libraries of the time but also above Oxford,
Cambridge, and other university libraries elsewhere and was on a
par or ahead of the royal libraries in Berlin, Dresden, Munich, Paris,
and the British Museum. It was not, however, Göttingen's size alone
which made it the best-known and most important library of the
last half of the eighteenth and the first quarter—at least—of the
nineteenth centuries. Lessing, while librarian (1770–1781) of the
famous ducal library at Wolfenbüttel, distinguished between libraries which have come into being or arisen more or less by chance
(*entstehende*), and those which have been laid out or planned
(*angelegte*). Most libraries, he claimed, belong to the first group,
but the better libraries, he suggested, are those of the second.[8] He
was making a point with respect to his own library, but he might
as well have been writing of Göttingen or Chicago or Johns Hopkins. Up to the founding of the Free University in Berlin and the

University of the Saarland after World War II, Göttingen was the most "planned" of all German university libraries.

The University of Göttingen, a true child of the Enlightenment, was founded by George II.[9] In its planning and early development it was the creation of Count Gerlach Adolph von Münchhausen (1688–1770), counsellor (*Geheimer Rat*) in the Hanoverian government. On the official opening in 1737, he was appointed chief administrative officer (*Kurator*). Münchhausen was, moreover, in a very real sense the spiritual father and the planner of the University Library. Whether his ideas for it derived, as has been suggested, from those of Leibniz,[10] sometimes called the first advocate of the concept of the modern scholarly library, is here immaterial.[11] The fact is that Münchhausen, a scholar and learned man, embodied in his plans for Göttingen major principles which Leibniz had either advanced or instituted during his tenure as librarian of the ducal library at Wolfenbüttel (1690–1716). Among these were very liberal regulations for use, (a Leibniz theory, but not a Leibniz practice!); regular budgets; scholarly quality, usefulness, and up-to-dateness of the collection; and book selection on a planned, regular, and international basis. Above all, and perhaps for the first time anywhere, Münchhausen consciously viewed the Library as an *indispensable* for the institution's teaching and research, as a part which could fulfill its essential role only by planned growth and regular nourishment. He intended the Library, in fact, to serve scholars everywhere in such a way that the reputation of the works they wrote would bring to the University a fame which none other could match. A man of enormous physical and intellectual energy, and of genuine vision, Münchhausen addressed himself to the problems of the Library, as to other parts of the University, with intelligence and unremitting zeal. He sought advice from the best men of the time. Plans for the Library were laid as early as 1732; by 1734, with the appointment of the first librarian, they were firmly established.[12] In 1735, two years before the official opening ceremonies, a book collection of 12,000 volumes had been acquired.[13] Münchhausen and the University were fortunate in the two men who principally guided the Library's destiny in its first three quarters of a century:

Johann Matthias Gesner, who had been librarian at the ducal library at Weimar and who served from 1734–1761, and, especially,
Christian Gottlob Heyne, whose librarianship, 1764–1812, fell just
short of a half century. Heyne, a founder of the new humanism and a
classical philologist of international reputation, was a born librarian.

Münchhausen supplied the administrative and financial support
—3,000–4,000 taler (perhaps $2,700–$3,600) a year for books in the
earliest years; the librarians an extraordinary zeal and enthusiasm,
combined with scholarly knowledge and discernment. The result
was that by 1763 the Library had acquired 60,000 volumes,[14] twice
as many as any other German university of the time, and three to
six times as many as most. The development in the succeeding years
was even more spectacular; by 1787 the collection numbered (by
actual count) 120,000 volumes, by 1812 around 200,000. The collections of its closest competitors at the time were not more than a
third as large. This is not, of course, to equate size with adequacy.
As we shall see, however, book selection was unquestionably better
at Göttingen than at any other university library of the day. Granted
equal or better selection, it is safe to assume that a larger collection
will satisfy more needs of more people than will a smaller one. Since
the early 1780s Göttingen had been adding between 2,000 and 2,200
volumes a year, so that by 1820 the holdings were in the neighbor-
hood of 238,000 volumes, and in 1838 around 300,000.[15]

It was not, however, as Pütter and dozens of the other producing
scholars of the time testified, its size alone that made Göttingen the
best known and very likely the best research library in the world.[16]
It was, in addition, two other facts, both unique for their time. One
was usability; the other, planned, systematic, thorough book selection on a continuing and international scale. As to the first of these,
it need only be noted here incidentally that almost from its beginning the library was open several hours a day, *six days a week* and
that every faculty member *and student* might use books in, or bor-
row them from, the Library at any time.[17] The intent of usability and
of usefulness, and liberal provisions for use were stated as early as
1761 in the regulations of that date.[18] (By contrast Harvard's regulations of the same period, that is, a century after the founding of
the College, permitted only certain students to use the Library, and

their borrowing was restricted to three books, once in three weeks, for three weeks. The borrowing and returning of books was limited to Fridays, 11 A.M. to 2 P.M.)

Heyne held the reins of book selection firmly in his own hands. For years he carried on a staggeringly voluminous correspondence with book dealers and publishers all over the world. The fame of the *Göttingische Gelehrte Anzeigen,* of which he became editor and to which, according to his biographer, he personally contributed enough reviews to make up twenty volumes,[19] became such that authors everywhere sought to have their works noticed in it. As a result, most of the best of the world's literature passed, as it were, under Heyne's own eyes. He was an indefatigable examiner of auction and book dealers' catalogs, and he bought everything he felt would benefit learning.

But the building of the collection was not simply library-centered. From the very beginning, the important journals, reviewing media, and dealers' catalogs were circulated to the professors, and desiderata were requested by them. They were, in fact, obliged to report important lacks.[20]

Heyne's view of his responsibilities and of the role and place of the Library are illuminating. In a 2,000-word letter written in 1809, in his eightieth year, to the Prefect he set forth his philosophy.

The Director, he writes, is required to take care of the great range of the literary and scholarly [business?] of the Library. To be able to do this, he has to survey the entire literary output of all periods. He must know at every point what of importance has been written, and whether it is already in the Library. Consequently, he must be familiar with the entire range not only of German but also of all European literature. To make this possible, a constant reading of journals and attention to important book auctions is required. The Librarian must be so familiar with new publications that he knows whether and which works belong in the scholarly program of the Library entrusted to him. The University Library, he writes, is no book store, no amateur library, and no court library. It contains works in all fields of learning and in all languages—everything, in short, of importance for scholarship and for those working in it. Only through observance of these principles could there have developed the superiority which has aroused admiration for the Library and made it the first of its kind in Europe. With respect to the newest literature of all European nations, he adds with perhaps pardonable pride, this Library may without immodesty be called the most sought after in the world.[21]

A year later Heyne expressed some of his views for a wider audience. Here he noted, first of all, the indispensable requirement of a liberal budget to make possible the regular purchase of the current publications of all countries. This is essential, Heyne said, if gaps are not to arise in this "invaluable treasure of human knowledge." Such gaps, he claims, would in time greatly impair the immeasurable value of the whole. He goes on to say that proper selection, rather than mere number of books is what makes real worth in a university library. Therefore, the uninterrupted, planned purchase of all important native and foreign publications produced by the development of knowledge is essential for a library with a scholarly plan.[22]

Of Göttingen's numerous other contributions to scholarly librarianship, notably in cataloging, organization, management, and staffing, this is not the place to speak. It must suffice to say here, by way of conclusion, that in one or more of these areas Göttingen strongly influenced the Astor Library, the Royal Library in Berlin, the British Museum, the Court Library in Munich, and the university libraries of Breslau, Harvard, Jena, Leipzig, Münster, Stuttgart, and Würzburg, among others. The full story of this influence has not been written; it deserves a comprehensive study.

That Göttingen after Heyne's death, and especially in the second and third quarters of the nineteenth century, fell on *relatively* poorer days was not the fault of the principles upon which it had been founded. The Library held fast to its guiding star: that the excellence of a library is achieved only through conscious, planned selection, supported by ample funds. The philosophy was repeated and underscored in 1833, during one of Göttingen's administratively and financially less happy periods, by Jacob Grimm, at the time one of those responsible for book selection. The elder Grimm, though in other respects perhaps less successful as a librarian than as a philologist, grammarian, lexicographer, and folklorist, fully recognized and accepted the principles upon which the Library's glory had been built.[23] Through mid-century (Table 1) to 1875 (Table 2) Göttingen remained the largest of the German university libraries.

Even this greatly abbreviated account of Göttingen's origin and earlier years will perhaps appear to the reader to give dispropor- tionate space to the story of a single institution. In justification, it may first be noted that the material in English on this important chapter of scholarly library history is very meager.[24] Much more important or valid justification, however, lies in the ground which Göttingen broke in respect to the building of its book collection. Nowhere else, at the time or earlier, are there to be found in com- bination, the stated, firm principles, and their actual implementa- tion, of a consistent, centrally administered book selection policy, designed to secure for a library every work of scholarly value, when- ever and wherever published; enormous library staff time expended toward this end; and ample, regular budgets to make the desired result possible. These factors (plus the very liberal provisions for use and usability) made of the Göttingen library an instrument that filled the needs of researchers and students as no other library of its day or before.

By the mid-nineteenth century, in contrast to the figures cited at the beginning of this chapter, the picture had substantially changed, at least for the German libraries, as Table 1 shows. It should be noted that the figures for the German institutions are not to be taken at face value; their beautifully rounded nature alone would make them suspect. However, for many we can, by adding the num- ber of individual, relatively small known gifts arrive at totals which, even without counting purchased books, approach the figures given. Thus, for Erlangen such known donations would alone come to around 100,000 volumes; exclusive of dissertations, the Library's total collection was only 120,000 volumes. Further, too many people knew enough of the status of individual libraries to permit the pub- lication of wildly improbable statistics. In any case, rough approxi- mations are all that is needed for the present purpose. The Ameri- can figures are probably fairly accurate. Most of the institutions were still very young, and their much smaller collections were more easily countable. Several had published inclusive catalogs—for ex-

TABLE 1

German and American University Libraries, 1850

Library	Volumes	Library	Volumes
Göttingen	350,000	Harvard c	84,200
Breslau a	300,000	Yale c	50,481
Munich	220,000	Brown	31,600
Heidelberg	200,000	South Carolina	18,400
Tübingen	200,000	Virginia	18,378
Erlangen	172,000	Princeton	16,000
Bonn	120,000	St. Louis	13,580
Rostock a	110,000–120,000	Columbia	12,740
Freiburg	100,000	Vermont	12,250
Giessen	100,000	North Carolina	11,847
Halle a	100,000	Rutgers	8,000
Marburg	100,000	Alabama	7,123
Würzburg	100,000	Pennsylvania	5,000
Jena a	80,000–100,000	Indiana	5,000
Leipzig a	90,000	Michigan	5,000
Kiel	80,000	Tennessee	4,500
Königsberg a	80,000	New York	4,000
Münster b	70,000	Mississippi	1,600
Greifswald a	50,000–60,000	Missouri	1,200
Berlin a	40,000		

a Universities now in East Germany are included for the sake of comparison and to complete the roster as it stood by 1850.

b Actually abolished as a university in 1818, but some academic activities continued and the library remained intact *in situ*, becoming part of the University Library when it was refounded in 1903.

c Included the collections in the law, theological, medical, and students' libraries.

Source: For the German libraries: Julius Petzholdt, *Handbuch Deutscher Bibliotheken* (Halle, Schmidt, 1853); for American libraries: Charles C. Jewett, *Notices of Public Libraries in the United States of America* (Washington, D.C., 1851).

ample, Pennsylvania (1829), Virginia (1828), Brown (1843), Yale (1823)—and some had made formal counts.

The chief reasons for the substantial growth of most of the German university libraries between the last of the eighteenth and the middle of the nineteenth centuries was not large increases in budgets; most of them remained very small. For example, Bonn (1819) had a budget of 1,500 taler ($1,350); Breslau (1812), 2,000 taler

($1,800); Halle (1823), 2,000 taler ($1,800); Leipzig (1821), 400 taler ($360); and Marburg in 1815 about 600 taler ($540) and in 1832 about 1,600 taler ($1,440).[25] The reasons lay, rather, in a series of three historical events: (1) the secularization of ecclesiastical institutions in 1773 (dissolution of the Jesuit Order), 1775, and 1782, which had libraries ranging from 10,000–80,000 volumes; (2) the Decree of the Imperial Deputation (*Reichsdeputationshauptschluss*) of 1803, which not only abolished many additional monasteries and other ecclesiastical jurisdictions, but also principalities and cities; and (3) a reform of university organization which, between 1798 and 1818, caused the abolishment of a score of weak and poor universities. Most of the remaining university libraries benefited from one or more of these events. Thus, simply as instances, libraries from monastery and other ecclesiastical institutions came to Breslau (about 70,000 volumes); Erlangen (over 12,000 volumes in 1803 and 13,000 in 1806); Heidelberg (60,000 volumes in 1828 alone, versus a total collection of about 20,000 in 1789); Freiburg (upward of thirty separate collections); Marburg, the Pauline Library at Münster, forerunner of the present university library; Munich (upward of 50,000 volumes); and Würzburg (9,000–10,000 volumes in 1803, versus a total collection of less than 20,000 a scant quarter of a century earlier). Among other universities which benefited were Berlin, Bonn, Halle, and Tübingen.[26]

Similarly, part of the library of the University of Helmstedt (founded 1576, dissolved 1809) went to Göttingen and Marburg; part of the library of the University of Rinteln (founded 1621, dissolved 1809) went to Marburg; part or all of the libraries of the universities of Frankfurt-an-der-Oder (founded 1506, dissolved 1811), of Altdorf (founded 1622, dissolved 1807), of Ingolstadt (founded 1472, removed to Landshut, 1800, to Munich, 1826), of Duisburg (founded 1655, dissolved 1818), and of Wittenberg (founded 1502, dissolved 1817) went to Breslau (about 28,000 volumes), to Erlangen (over 8,000 volumes), to Munich (40,000 volumes), to Bonn (6,000 volumes), and to Halle (10,000 volumes).

The collections of many, many other nonuniversity libraries were also enriched in like manner. It should be noted, too, that some of the greatest treasures, and much of the general strength, of all these libraries, in medieval manuscripts and early printed books also came to the libraries from the same sources.

A further, often equally and sometimes more significant cause of the libraries' growth, in the first decades of the nineteenth century was the donations, chiefly of professors' and other scholars' collections, which they received. Many of these donations would be considered large in absolute terms in any day; for the time, some of them were stupendous. Thus, simply for example, Bonn, a collection of 8,700 volumes; Erlangen, one of 25,000 volumes (versus total holdings of about 30,000 toward the end of the nineteenth century); Würzburg, 15,000 volumes (total holdings of about 20,000 volumes near the close of the nineteenth century); and Leipzig, four collections alone totaling 43,000 volumes between 1813 and 1840; in 1789 Leipzig's entire collection consisted of less than half this amount.

University libraries everywhere have, of course, been benefited enormously from their earliest days by gifts. The German libraries were no exception, and their early collections, like those in the Colonies and the United States, derived almost entirely from this source. It seems unlikely, however, that any libraries anywhere, as a group, received gifts greater in size compared to existing collections than did the German universities between the end of the eighteenth and the middle of the nineteenth centuries.

It is not too much to say that these various windfalls usually at least doubled, often tripled, and in a few instances quadrupled the libraries' holdings within a period of about sixty years. Many of the collections, however, particularly those from some of the monasteries, which thus came to the libraries, contained masses of literature bearing little relationship to the academic needs of the time. Certainly nothing in the way of selection or planned collection building was involved in any of these large additions to the university libraries, and there is almost no evidence that any of the material, except duplicates, was discarded.

By the middle of the nineteenth century only a quarter of the German libraries had collections representing as much as 4 to 5 percent of the total world book publishing output up to that year.[27] We cannot say with any certainty how adequate these libraries were for the needs of the day. Considerable contemporary evidence suggests that most of them were considered quite inadequate. The largely unplanned nature, the very high percentage of gift material, and the relatively small size of all but a few, tend to lead to the same conclusion. (Today it would certainly require a collection of more than a million volumes, without taking journals into account, to constitute 5 percent of the world publishing output.)

The American libraries were, of course, much less well off, but then, none was a research or university library. Indeed, our first real university was, in 1850, a quarter of a century away from being founded. The American list in Table 1 is interesting from a quite different point of view. A number of the major American state universities—California, Illinois, Minnesota, and Texas, for example—had not yet been founded or, like Wisconsin (1849) had just begun, and many of the most distinguished post-revolutionary private institutions—Chicago, Cornell, Duke, Johns Hopkins, Northwestern, Rochester, and Stanford—were also not yet born. Michigan, Missouri, Virginia, and Indiana were all less than forty years old.

Nonetheless, it was in this century that book-collecting policy, both in Germany—Göttingen being the earlier exception—and in America began to be formulated. In Germany, indeed, policy on the nature of the materials to be collected became firm. One of the earliest promulgated and comprehensive statements is to be found in the Erlangen Directive of 1826. Twelve sections are specifically concerned with book selection. The first notes that the University Library, as an indispensable literary aid to the University's aims, is to promote the spirit of true science and art, and to serve as a comprehensive, planned repository of their works. Consequently, Section 2 goes on to say, the Library will not acquire, even as gift, insignificant or dispensable works, or those which simply serve to satisfy curiosity, or the wishes of the beginner or the unlearned. Section 4 directs that works of superior and continuing value shall not be neglected in any field, and that such works which are lacking in any field shall be acquired at the earliest opportunity. According to Section 6 originals are to be preferred to translations, and the latter deserve a place in the Library only when they have a specific interest for art or science. Further, works which simply help a beginner to understand an author are not to be acquired. Finally, Section 10 directs that consideration regularly be given only to classical works of all nations, particularly Germany; outside of such works only those books shall be acquired as have retained a continuing significance as a result either of their origin or of their effect. Other sections remark the indispensable nature of certain kinds of reference works (5); require the immediate acquisition of works likely to become rapidly scarce (9); and call for the collection of important foreign journals (11).[28]

Even earlier, though in this respect not nearly so comprehensive a Regulation, is that of Königsberg. Here the faculty is specifically directed to limit its proposals for books to major works and to those which have a scholarly purpose; unimportant works, those which every professor can acquire for himself [!] and those which serve only the ends of entertainment are to be excluded. Above all, the guiding viewpoint should be, that no important scholarly work be lacking in the collection.[29]

The same basic view is expressed in the Rostock Directive of a few years later. Books shall be acquired which offer sources and aids for scholarly research or which contain important results of fundamental studies and observations. On the other hand, textbooks and similar writings, which teachers and students should have in their personal libraries, and books of entertainment or of ephemeral political interest are not to be acquired.[30]

Kiel, in a Regulation of 1826, directed its Commission toward: "Acquisition of works which have a general scholarly interest. . . . Such writings as have been epoch-making in scholarship in every period, and in general only works of lasting value, must be at hand." [31] This Regulation remained substantially unchanged until 1879.

These examples may suffice to define the general policy. The essential commitment was to the scholarly, the scientific, and to research with a corresponding nonacceptance of teaching, entertainment, and introductory literature. Fundamentally, this remains the policy of the German university libraries today.

Two further concepts, that of "completeness" or "universality," and that of balanced, objective, collection-building were established.

It may be said at once that available funds were nowhere sufficient for anything like a full realization of the first policy; it is almost equally certain that the ways in which book funds were allocated often did violence to the second. Nonetheless, formal expression was repeatedly given to both ideas, and there is considerable evidence to suggest that serious effort was made to implement them.

Thus, as instances, the Breslau Regulations of 1815: "In the acquisition of new works . . . consideration is to be given to the greatest possible bibliographic completeness of every field, without neglect of some fields or preference for others." [32] The phrase "without neglect of some fields or preference for others" is a much quoted one in the German literature of the subject. Precisely identical wording is found in the Bonn Regulations of four years later.[33] At Erlangen: "Works which have a superior and lasting value shall not be neglected in any field; and major works, lacking in a field, shall be acquired when the opportunity presents itself." [34]

The Library Commission at Giessen was instructed to achieve a proper relationship between the demand of the several scholarly departments and the funds available for selection. The Commission was also to bring about the greatest possible bibliographical completeness of every field, and to avoid neglect of some fields or preference for others.[35] At Kiel the Commission was also directed to develop the different scholarly fields and subfields in the most uniform manner possible while, at the same time, giving earliest attention to those fields which most required completeness.[36]

In two other respects book-selection policy for the German university libraries did not become firm, or at least universally accepted, in the nineteenth century. These related elements of policy were the responsibility for selection and the control of book funds. Until well into the period, beginning in the 1870s, which saw the acceptance of the full-time professional librarian, much of the administrative responsibility for managing the library, including authority for book selection, was, in many universities, placed in the hands of a library commission. Kiel's Commission, one of the earliest, established in 1793, had wide authority including, for nearly three quarters of a century, that for book selection. This was accomplished by dividing the fields of knowledge among the members of the

Commission and making them responsible for ordering books in their fields and for ascertaining faculty wishes. Here, as in similar situations elsewhere, the librarian had responsibility for *acquiring* books, but not for *selecting* them.[37] Similar bodies were established at Göttingen—where a commission was created as a measure of expediency and compromise following Heyne's death—at Tübingen, Giessen, and at other universities. At Giessen, everything concerned with the acquisition of books was subject to the deliberations of a Library Commission appointed for that purpose. The members of the Commission were responsible for recommending the acquisition of books in their fields of knowledge to the body as a whole which had the final decision. Here, as elsewhere, desiderata note books, in which professors could write the names of desired items, were made available—as they still commonly are—for the teaching staff whose wishes and needs Commission members were directed to discover and fulfill.[38]

Freiburg's Commission had, from 1830 to 1870, virtually complete authority over the Library, including book acquisition, although it was expected that professors would make proposals (*Vorschläge*) for titles to be purchased.[39]

Further, at many institutions during a large part of the century, book funds were apportioned to the faculties and departments. Erlangen early adopted such a policy, dividing its book funds: two-tenths for binding; one-tenth each for the faculties of theology, law, and medicine; three-tenths for the faculty of philosophy; and two-tenths to the librarian for journals, newspapers, and other general works.[40]

At Königsberg, of a total book fund of 2,444 taler ($2,200), the faculties of theology, law, and medicine were each appropriated 200 taler ($180); the philosophical faculty 1,075 taler ($968), with thirteen suballotments specified, etc.; and the librarians 319 taler ($287) for the purchase of necessary literary apparatus (*literarischen Apparats*) and larger works. The faculties were given exclusive determination of the books to be purchased from the allotted funds; book selection or acquisition in any way was not mentioned among the list of duties of the librarians.[41]

Rostock's book budget of 1,500 taler ($1,350) was divided 950 taler ($855) among thirteen faculties and departments and 550 taler ($495) to the Commission. The sum at the disposal of the Commission was for filling in gaps, the purchase of multi-interest works, encyclopedias, journals, society publications, etc. "The Library office may never use for Library purposes any part of a (departmental) appropriation without the knowledge and written permission of its administrator." [42]

Giessen's book fund was divided into ten parts; the Ministry determining, as often as necessary, on the basis of the Library's collection, the status of the several fields, literary production, and the needs of the university, the proportion to be allocated. [43]

As noted earlier, both the commission, or other nonlibrary-centered book-selection authority, and the allotment of book funds were prevalent throughout the nineteenth century. The policy of allotment persisted beyond 1900. Reference may be made, therefore, to some of the latest and most refined examples. Although the arbitrary chronological division of the study must here be somewhat violated, the violation is more apparent than real. In the German view, as we shall see in Chapter III, apportionment of book funds belongs to an earlier rather than a modern philosophy, that is, to the nineteenth century. Erlangen, as late as 1903, had a Regulation which remained in force until 1927 and which allocated total library funds one-ninth each to the theological, law, and medical faculties; one-sixth to each of two divisions of the philosophical faculty; the remaining one-third was used by the librarian for administrative costs, binding, bibliography, "general" works, newspapers, general learned journals, and reference works. [44] On which Paul Schwenke, then editor of the *Zentralblatt für Bibliothekswesen* commented: "The regulation preserves the old allocation system which rends the Library in separate parts and makes every healthy acquisition policy impossible." [45] Certainly, in this respect, Erlangen's policy had remained substantially the same for just a century.

At Rostock at the same time the Regulation called for twenty-one departmental allocations, ranging from 140 M for agriculture-forestry through 450 M for physics and 600 M for political science to 1,200 M, 1,700 M, and 1,920 M for theology, law, and medicine respectively.[46] Rostock's policy, too, was unaltered for more than sixty-five years.

Giessen, also in 1904, had much refined its policy of 1837, and, going perhaps as far in the direction of detailed division as any American library, broke its book funds into forty-fifths, political science, oriental literature, and theology, for instance, receiving one, two, and four forty-fifths respectively of the total.[47]

These were among the last examples of the system and by 1906, in fact, Milkau wrote, no doubt referring to them, "In the university libraries, with a few exceptions which seem very strange in the framework of modern librarianship, the old, fatal, frittering away of funds through division among the faculties or subject representatives has been done away with." [48]

Meanwhile, that is, during the nineteenth century, policy was also being formed in the United States. Not unnaturally, in view of the later development of the American institutions as real universities, it was slower in forming than in Germany.

To be sure, Cogswell at Harvard in the 1820s, on the basis of his observations at Göttingen, offered proposals for systematic, comprehensive, and intensive collecting.[49] But in this respect Cogswell was unsuccessful, and it was not until a generation later, under the librarianship of Sibley, that the kind of program Cogswell advocated came into being. He wrote:

The Library is not more used for reading than it is for literary, genealogical, historical, statistical, philological, philosophical, scientific, and other investigations. It is the reservoir from which all minds at the University are mainly to be supplied. *No limits can be set to its wants.* . . . The field of intellectual labor is now so broad, and so carefully and extensively cultivated, that applications are made . . . for books, pamphlets, and papers, which by a superficial, one-sided inquirer would be considered worthless. . . . Biographers and historians ask for ephemeral pamphlets, newspapers, manuscript diaries and letters, relating to the times and persons of which they write. Macaulay cites old almanacs. Some American Hallam or Sismondi will want to examine the school-books of the last and present centuries, to obtain a general idea of their character and of the early education of the country. . . . *I think it would be well if it were generally known that there was never anything printed of which we should not be grateful for one copy.*[50] (italics added)

The Harvard Visiting Committee did not immediately agree, and held the view that "documentary matter, accumulated in a desultory or fragmentary state . . . though useful for reference and occasional researches, does not constitute a necessary portion of the didactic or illustrative materials of education." [51] But its position of two years later was a little different.

It is, indeed, doubted by some, whether it is right to stimulate the building up of so immense a Library as that of Harvard . . . now bids fair, at no very distant day, to become. On this point the Committee feel no hesitation. They believe that the . . . Library . . . is destined to grow indefinitely. . . . Books that are read are made by the aid of those which only bookmakers ever open. . . . If society is susceptible of unlimited progress, then the multiplying of "first sources" of knowledge cannot be carried too far.[52]

Whatever the views of the Committee, Sibley in fact, unquestionably collected extensively and intensively the "ephemera" and nonbook materials, as well as books, that he saw as essential to a university library. His successor, Winsor, was like-minded, declaring that "nothing that is printed, no matter how trivial at the time, but may be some day in demand, and, viewed in some relations, helpful to significant results." [53] Winsor's president, Charles William Eliot, writing a little later, in 1891, supported his views, at least to this extent, "the university that undertakes to provide for the wants of advanced students in all departments absolutely requires an immense collection of books, and must have the means of buying every year all the really good books that are issued in the civilized world." [54]

A little later Yale's librarian, Addison Van Name, was appealing to alumni to send all kinds of local publications to the university library, and James Hulme Canfield, of Columbia, just after the turn of the century, wrote, "There is a constant demand, not for books about sources, but for the sources themselves." [55] Even more specifically, to round out the picture—though it violates slightly the chronology—he expressed the belief that, "it is hardly possible to bring together too many aids or to make any collection too large or complete . . . the University must collect largely—as largely as possible—in every field of knowledge." [56]

The faculty committee, with varying powers so far as the book collection was concerned, also became prevalent in the nineteenth century. Virginia's, first appointed in 1836, had both the power to approve faculty requests *and* to select general titles which did not fall within a single instructional field.[57] Book selection, here as elsewhere was, and continued to be primarily, and sometimes exclusively, a faculty function.[58] Policy in this respect appears usually, as in Stanford's case, to have "been entirely a matter of practice" without "specific enunciation of responsibility for it." [59]

At Minnesota, too, there were no "official statements or directives upon which . . . selection policy rests." [60] However, at Stanford and at some other institutions, authority for the allocation of funds to schools and departments was formally vested in a library committee, board, or council. Such allocation inevitably meant, of course, major if not exclusive book selection authority and responsibility in the hands of the faculty. Allocated funds could generally be spent only with the specific consent of the department head or a designated representative.

At Cornell, as another instance: "It shall be the duty of the Library Council to apportion the book funds between the various departments of instruction . . . and to recommend and submit to the Trustees for their approval all questions pertaining to the apportionment of funds. . . . The Librarian and President have power to approve orders, signed by the Professors at the head of the departments." [61] The stated duties of the librarian, not surprisingly, include no reference to book selection or collection building.

Whether or not written policy was promulgated makes little difference. The fact is, that institutions founded before 1900, as well as those of later date, generally developed the practice of allocating most of their book funds and generally relied upon faculty and faculty committees to a greater or lesser extent.

The foregoing references and discussion may be sufficient to point up the parallels between selection and collecting policy and its development in Germany and the United States in the nineteenth century. In both countries, in Germany earlier than in America, emphasis came to be laid upon comprehensive collecting, to as

complete an extent as possible and upon collecting for research
needs. In both countries—in Germany, generally, for most of the
century—book funds were allocated to departments or faculties
and—in Germany, again, for the greater part of the period—
responsibility for *selection* was mostly not in the hands of the
library but was vested in the faculty or a committee or both. The
major difference, considered in detail in Chapter IV, lay in a more
restricted German view of what constitutes research materials or
materials for research needs. The subsequent diverging basic
policies of selection of the two countries, chiefly a development of
the twentieth century, are discussed in the succeeding chapter.

If we move ahead a quarter of a century from 1850, we find the
situation shown in Table 2. The student of library history is not
greatly surprised by the figures in the right hand column. He knows
that the first true university in the United States had not yet been
founded, that real library strength depended upon demand from
graduate faculties, and that "it was not until 1900 that graduate
schools began to emerge from among our colleges and state and
municipal universities." [62] The earliest graduate schools, as at Johns
Hopkins (1876), Clark (1889), and Chicago (1893), were only a
little earlier than this and, aside chiefly from law and medicine,
most American professional schools were begun after 1875. Bishop
observed years ago that "the goal of adequate provision of the
materials for advanced research . . . is a development of the last
seventy-five years, perhaps even the last forty years." [63] He meant
precisely, 1863–1898. Wilson has noted that at North Carolina, "From
1886 to 1901 the additions to the collections were largely for the
support of undergraduate teaching," and that the establishment of
the Graduate School in 1904 was a major factor in the formulation
of policies emphasizing the collection of materials for graduate
study and research.[64]

By no stretch of the imagination could it be maintained that any
American institution in 1875, with the possible exception of Harvard, had a "university library." The mean increase in volumes from
1850 to 1875 of the thirteen libraries which appear on both Tables
1 and 2 is 29,200, or 1,168 per year per library. The median is 823
volumes. If one omits Harvard and Yale, the mean drops to 628

TABLE 2

German and American University Libraries, 1875

Library	Volumes	Library	Volumes
Göttingen	400,000	Harvard [c]	227,650
Heidelberg	370,000	Yale [c]	114,000
Leipzig [a]	346,000	Brown	45,000
Breslau [a]	337,100	Princeton	41,500
Strassburg [a]	300,000	Virginia	40,000
Munich	283,500	Cornell	39,000
Tübingen	278,000	Columbia	34,790
Freiburg	250,000	Northwestern	30,000
Königsberg [a]	220,000	South Carolina	28,250
Würzburg	198,000	Georgetown	28,000
Jena [a]	180,000	Michigan	27,500
Bonn	180,000	Pennsylvania	25,573
Erlangen	160,000	St. Louis	25,000
Berlin [a]	155,000	North Carolina	22,207
Giessen	150,000	Georgia	21,600
Kiel	150,000	Vermont	16,021
Rostock [a]	140,000	Louisiana	15,000
Marburg	120,000	Missouri	13,400
Münster [b]	100,000	Rochester	12,000
Halle [a]	100,000	California	12,000
Greifswald [a]	70,000	Duke (Trinity) [c]	10,900
		Illinois [d]	10,600
		Minnesota [d]	10,000
		Notre Dame [d]	10,000
		Iowa State University [c, d]	8,823
		Wisconsin [c, d]	8,563
		New York University [d]	3,500
		Kansas [d]	2,448
		Nebraska [d]	1,400
		Ohio [d]	1,000

[a] Universities now in East Germany and Strassburg are included for the sake of comparison and to complete the roster as it stood by 1875.

[b] Actually abolished as a university in 1818, but some academic activities continued and the library remained intact in situ, becoming part of the University Library when it was refounded in 1903.

[c] Included the collections in the law, theological, medical, and students' libraries.

[d] Institutions founded by 1875, the libraries of which later grew to relative major size, are included for comparison with Tables 3, 4, 5, or 6.

Source: For the German libraries: Julius Petzholdt, Adressbuch der Bibliotheken Deutschlands mit Einschluss von Österreich-Ungarn und der Schweiz (Dresden, Schönfeld, 1875); for American libraries: United States Department of the Interior, Bureau of Education, Public Libraries in the United States of America (Washington, D.C., Government Printing Office, 1876).

volumes per year per library, with a median of 488 volumes. With the exception of these two, regular book funds during most of the period were miniscule or nonexistent. Harvard, always unusually fortunate in attracting cash gifts for book purchases, increased its annual expenditures from about $1,000 in 1853 to about $7,800 in 1873, and was far in the lead.

The figures in the left hand column of Table 2 are perhaps more surprising. The mean yearly increase, 1850–1875, of the libraries is 3,368 volumes (median 2,670 volumes), almost three times the figure (1,168 volumes) for the American institutions. But by 1875, if we accept Iwinski's estimates, world book production may have totaled something like six and a half million volumes.[65] Only four of the German libraries held as many as 5 percent of this total, and less than half of them held as many as 3 percent, even ignoring bound journals. Other libraries had strong basic collections and outstanding wealth in some fields, but it seems probable that not more than half of the total group was capable of supporting intensive research along the whole horizontal range of the universities' programs. At this time, too, as we shall see in Chapter III, the development of large and numerous institute libraries was still in the future.

CHAPTER III

Modern Selecting and Collecting

Before considering other aspects of modern book selection and collecting policy, brief allusion, at least, should be made to the idea of completeness and its general abandonment in this century. Both in Germany and in the United States, as we have seen in the preceding chapter, the idea, at least as an ideal, came generally to be accepted during the nineteenth century. It persisted, in fact, in some quarters well into the twentieth century. Even when relinquished, abandonment was often grudging and reluctant. But the idea of completeness was eventually everywhere given up, as countless annual reports and articles abundantly testify.[1] The idea was given up as its practical impossibility came to be realized. The cause was the enormous proliferation of knowledge and the resulting vast increase in publication. In respect to the abandonment of the idea of completeness, the policy in Germany and the United States remained closely parallel. In several other respects it diverged radically.

The administrative and "legal" responsibility for book selection today in the "main" or "central" library of the German university, (and in most university libraries of the Continent), rests solely in the hands of the librarian and his staff, who have absolute control of the book funds. In the United States categorical generalization is not possible. Speaking in broad terms, however, it may be said that, although the responsibility administratively and legally may, and frequently does reside in the library, it has generally been taken over, as a practical matter, by the faculty. The actual selection of books is largely carried out by the same two groups—by librarians in Germany, by faculty members in the United States. Redenbacher, Bauhuis, and others strongly imply that this is— except for reference titles, materials of general reading interest, and works cutting across two or more fields of interest—virtually one hundred percent the case in America.[2] The generalization is as accurate as most generalizations, but, as we shall see, the actual practice is not so black and white as is generally supposed.

The German position is based upon the premise that the books should be selected by subject specialists (*Referenten*) on the staff of the library, upon which rests the responsibility for building the collection. The American position is based upon the premise that the books for the library should be selected primarily by members of the teaching staff, since it is they who best know (a) the subject fields and their literatures, (b) the faculty and other research needs, and (c) the needs of students. On the surface, each philosophy appears to be logically defensible. In practice, and to a degree in theory, both systems may be shown to have serious weaknesses which have worked to the disadvantage of scholarship. The following discussion considers the two systems from both the theoretical and practical points of view.

POLICY AND PRACTICE IN GERMANY

Since well before the beginning of the twentieth century, the German university has maintained two separate and completely autonomous library operations: a "main" or "central" library (*Hauptbibliothek*) and a group of seminar and institute libraries. The main library, largely independent of the university administration, receives its funds from the state, which is constitutionally responsible for the establishment and maintenance of libraries. The expenditure of these funds, and the selection of all books for the main library, rest entirely in the hands of the librarian and his staff. The selection of books for, and the administration and management of, the libraries of the institutes and seminars, are wholly under the authority of their directors.[3]

Library Subject Specialists and Book Selection Responsibility. Commencing about the turn of the twentieth century, the university library began to develop the present departmental or subject specialist system (*Referatsystem*). The basic feature of the system is the assignment of book selection and book collection-building responsibility to a corps of academically and professionally qualified library staff members. This responsibility, however, it must be stressed, pertains only to the university library, and extends in no manner whatever to book selection for, or the book collections of, the numerous, often large, independent seminar and institute libraries.

The *Referatsystem* of the German scholarly library, though essentially a development of the twentieth century, was at least to some degree implied at Breslau as early as 1815 where the "inspection and judgment of the members of the [library] meetings" (*"Einsicht und Beurtheilung der Konferenzmitglieder"*) of new books is referred to, and where the supposition is made that responsibility for some book selection in specific fields may be placed upon library staff specialists.[4] Almost precisely the same phraseology appears in the Bonn directive of four years later.[5] Both of these, as well as numerous later regulations, show, in content and language, the strong influence of Schleiermacher's famous *Reglement* for the Royal Library in Berlin.[6]

Not until the early twentieth century did university libraries generally have sufficiently large staffs to establish the system. Two other important changes had occurred. Around the 1870s, through the efforts of Ernst Förstermann, librarian of the Royal Library at Dresden, Robert von Mohl, somewhat earlier at Tübingen, Anton Klette [7] at Jena, and others, the professor-librarian began to be a thing of the past and academic librarianship as a profession came to be recognized.[8] As an unfortunate result, however, university library commissions, similar to the American senate or faculty library committee, were then almost everywhere established, if not already in existence, and were granted great administrative powers. Although the commissions were generally, in the words of the Göttingen statute, given "the task of producing a continuing relationship between the teaching staff . . . and the Library administration, and of exerting an appropriate influence on . . . suitable accessions," [9] they performed the first task little or not at all, and the second one badly. As Leyh notes, "Proof that commissions have substantially furthered libraries has not been brought forward." [10] Nonetheless, as we have seen in the previous chapter, commissions were, almost everywhere, invested with administrative authority, including the area of book selection. The battle against administrative commissions and for the independence of the librarian in professional matters was not fully won until the turn of the century.[11] (In Germany today the commission, like the library committee in America, is very largely advisory and supportive; it is frequently almost completely inactive.)

With conditions thus favorable, and with book production now far too large to be handled by one man as it was in Heyne's day —and later—the German university libraries proceeded very quickly to establish the *Referatsystem*.[12] Münster incorporated it from the date of the Library's reconstitution in 1903, and most libraries had inaugurated it by the end of the 1920s. A typical statement of its advantages and workings is one from Freiburg, where the system was introduced in 1926.[13] So basic did it come to be held that it was sometimes incorporated into formal orders or statutes as that of Tübingen, 1929.[14]

In the typical German university library, the corps of subject specialists (*Referenten*), who have been called "the hoplites of the library," [15] averages eight individuals—the actual range being from four to fifteen. All hold the doctorate in an academic subject, have had about two years of library education, and have passed a state examination. Each is assigned responsibility for the selection of materials, both current and older, and for general building of the collections in several subject fields.[16]

The concentration and coordination of book selection for the German *university library* in the hands of a few individuals having specific responsibility, advanced subject knowledge, and immediate and constant access to all kinds of bibliographic apparatus constitute a very great asset. The *Referenten* have a firm awareness of library policy. They have, as well, an intimate and personal knowledge of the existing collections in their fields—a knowledge seldom matched on the other side of the Atlantic. They have, finally, an understanding of the relationship of their fields to others and to the world of learning in general. For these reasons, book buying for the German university library is a planned, purposeful activity, having balance and coordination.

A system like the *Referenten* has at least two other strong advantages which merit mention. It provides library staff subject specialists with the opportunity of keeping abreast of work in their fields and of participating in the most important work of the library, that is, building its collections. The system is thus to the greatest degree a builder of staff morale and *esprit de corps*. Secondly, by its maintenance of a group of staff members with the highest academic education, the library is more likely to be viewed by the faculty as a genuinely scholarly enterprise than where this is not the case. Although, as we shall see, the average German university professor virtually ignores the university library, he does hold it to be a scholarly activity. The important point here, however, is not application to a particular country but rather the general concept. The professor will tend to have more confidence in the library staff member who is his academic equal.

The weaknesses of the system are of three kinds. The first two have to do with its internal implementation. In the first place, the corps of subject specialists is simply too small (chiefly a matter of funds) to perform its task properly. Thus, over and over again, one finds a single individual with responsibility for a group, such as, Orientalia, music, general language, and philosophy; psychology, philosophy, pedagogy, and English philology; or geography, geology, mineralogy, paleontology, oceanography, ethnology, geochemistry, geophysics, and hydrology. In most cases the literature of two or perhaps three such fields is all that one individual could be expected to know sufficiently well. Combined with the size of the present obligation is the fact that the specialists commonly are able to devote only about ten to fifteen, occasionally up to twenty hours a week to the entire spectrum of selection. Administrative responsibilities in acquisitions, cataloging, or reader services, and so on, and the descriptive cataloging of books in their fields, take up the rest of their time. The book selection responsibilities of the *Referenten* include (1) reading thirty to fifty major subject journals, (2) checking the principal regularly issued bibliographies, such as, *Publishers' Weekly, Bibliographie de la France, Deutsche Bibliographie, Deutsche Nationalbibliographie, Börsenblatt für den Deutschen Buchhandel, Bibliographie de Belgique, Berliner Titel-*

drucke, Der Schweizer Buchhandel, Svensk Bokförteckning, and *Nieuwe Uitgave in Nederland,* which, with other like titles, are regularly circulated to all *Referenten;* (3) reading reviews in subject journals and in such general media as the *Times Literary Supplement;* (4) checking second-hand catalogs and titles in them against desiderata files and/or the card catalogs; (5) personally examining up to a hundred new books, mostly German, each week; and (6) making up annotated recommendation slips. The task is too great. The only way the *Referent* even begins to perform it is by doing a large part of his checking out-of-hours in the evenings and on weekends at home. Statistics kept at Tübingen show that the *Referenten* spend, on the average, almost twenty hours per week or a little less than half of their normal working hours on book selection; the figure does not, however, include time spent at home which, in one case at least, amounted to about fifteen hours per week.

About a quarter of the *Referenten* with whom this question was discussed felt that to do adequately the entire book selection task for all their fields would require all of the time of their normal work week. A strong majority felt they would need twice as much time as they were able to spend; *all* felt that they needed at least some more time. Chief librarians, when pressed, generally concede that the task should require half or more of the time of the *Referenten* but grant that their other responsibilities make this impossible.

All of this book-selection activity culminates, in all but five of the eighteen libraries, in weekly, or biweekly, book-selection meetings, literally, in German, "purchase sessions" (*Kaufsitzungen*).[17] At these meetings, chaired by the librarian or his deputy, each of the *Referenten,* in turn, presents the titles and books he has considered since the last meeting. German books are usually sent to the library on approval, have been examined by the *Referenten,* and are on display at the meetings. Foreign titles are generally presented on the basis of such information as the *Referent* has about the author and probable value of the work. The 150–250 titles commonly taken up at each meeting are presented by the six to twelve *Referenten,* each thus offering something like 15 to 35 titles in the fields for which he is responsible. The presentation is rapid and brief, with little or no comment by the others present who, of course, know neither these titles nor the fields involved. The *Kaufsitzung*, therefore, rarely vetos the judgment of a *Referent*. Where *Kaufsitzungen* are not held, titles recommended for purchase by the *Referenten* are customarily submitted to the librarian, and/or his deputy, for review and approval.

A somewhat different system exists, chiefly because of a gross lack of personnel, at Erlangen, Munich, and Würzburg. In these libraries, with only four or five *Referenten*-qualified staff members each, it is patently impossible to divide formally the numerous fields of learning. Book selection is performed chiefly by the librarian who spends between fifteen and fifty hours a week on title-by-title selection from general bibliographies, publishers' announcements, and general reviewing media. These materials are also reviewed to some degree by the other staff members who additionally are sent catalogs, etc., in the fields of their subject specializations and are free to recommend for purchase any titles that come to their attention in any field. It is estimated that the librarian and his staff together spend a total of from fifty-five to eighty hours per week on all aspects of book selection. Faculty selection activity is estimated at 1–3 percent of the total number of volumes purchased. The chief differences, then, between this variant and the system operating in most libraries are (1) that the subject fields are not formally apportioned to members of the staff and (2) that by far the largest portion of actual selection is performed by the chief librarian.

The practicality of holding *Kaufsitzungen* under today's circumstances seems questionable. A library which is adding, for example, 15,000 new purchased titles a year would have to consider in a probable maximum of forty-five weekly sessions, about 330 titles per session. Even if one assumes, generously, that one half of these are obvious "musts," or rejects, requiring no deliberation, it is apparent that in such a situation little more than the reading of a list is possible; any real consideration of individual titles is quite out of the question. In 1958–1959 the libraries actually added an average of 12,645 new purchased titles, including those bought with funds provided by the *Deutsche Forschungsgemeinschaft*.[18]

Under present conditions and procedures, the general value of the *Kaufsitzung,* when weighed against its cost, may also be seriously doubted. It is most unlikely that more than a handful of all the titles considered in a meeting will be generally remembered by the members of the group even a few weeks after the meeting. Consequently, the argument that the *Kaufsitzung* provides all members of the group with an opportunity to become familiar with materials being added to the library appears weak. Against this picture of dubious benefit must be weighed very substantial costs to the library. Assuming a group of ten individuals, including librarian and assistant librarian, an average weekly salary of 315 DM, a work week of forty-five hours, and weekly *Kaufsitzungen* of two hours, the cost to the library is about 140 DM per week, or 6,300 DM for forty-five meetings a year. This is approximately $1,600, which might buy four hundred additional books, or catalog twice that many.[19]

Since 1957, the near-median size library of Münster has kept statistics which make possible another kind of analysis.[20] The costs of two series of *Kaufsitzungen* were about a third and nearly a quarter the cost of the books purchased. A total of 2,514 volumes was bought as the result of thirty-four meetings, an average of 74 volumes per meeting.

At Tübingen, one of the three largest libraries holding *Kaufsitzungen,* ten *Referenten* meet weekly for about three hours, and on the average fifty to sixty titles are purchased as the result of each session. The cost figures are, therefore, approximately the same.

Advocates of the *Kaufsitzungen* offer a further argument in their support. It is maintained that the sessions, by providing an opportunity for the *Referenten* to meet together, are a strong builder of staff morale. It may be suggested that the many and obvious advantages of staff meetings can be derived as well and more profitably from gatherings devoted to a discussion of the important issues and problems which university libraries constantly face.

The serious financial straits of most of the German libraries suggest that the costs of *Kaufsitzungen* might better be diverted to other uses.[21] Had such a diversion been in effect over the past ten, twenty, or thirty years, the scholarly resources of many of the libraries would have been materially increased. Further, it is exceedingly doubtful that the nature of the books actually selected for purchase would have been significantly different from what it was.

A second handicap to the internal implementation of the system lies in the great difficulty the libraries have in maintaining their corps of *Referenten* for certain fields such as Oriental languages and literature, the Near East, and the physical and biological sciences. Most libraries have at least one vacancy at any given time. All, of course, suffer occasional staff illness of some duration. What does the library do? It temporarily assigns the field in question to someone else. But the assignee is almost always not a specialist in the field, and seldom has interest in it. Further, though most of the *Referenten,* members of the "higher service," (*höheren Dienst*), would be quite capable of "working up" such a common field as Germanics, English, or Romance languages and literature, which generally present no staffing problem, no one can "work up" on short notice Sinology or the physical sciences. The problem is partly inherent—Japanologists, Sinologists, scientists, and some other kinds of experts are in short supply—partly a matter of inadequate salary scales, and partly, perhaps, a result of the fact that there are only two library schools (at Cologne and Munich) for all of Germany preparing for the *höheren Dienst*. But this problem, and the related one of overall normal size of the corps of *Referenten,* will have to be solved before the *Referatsystem* will be as successful as it should be and as most German university librarians think it is.

Some official opinion and professional belief exist, however, to the effect that the number of *Referenten* should be not fewer than twelve, (including the librarian and assistant librarian who typically have selection responsibility for a subject field), and that a better dispersion should obtain than is generally the case.[22] As of the time of this study, only five libraries had even as many as twelve

Referenten. Redenbacher, in discussing the system, expresses the judgment:

It is obviously meaningfully practicable only when a sufficient number of librarians is available, and their fields of subject specialization and interest display an appropriate dispersion. Before the system can be carried out in its full range and with all desirable results, most German university libraries will need to increase substantially their scholarly personnel in the light of the different subject fields.[23]

Institute and Departmental Libraries. The third, and graver problem of the German university—note, not simply "university library"—with respect to its book resources and their selection relates to a different matter. This is the traditional, deeply entrenched system of seminars and institutes.[24] Their earliest origins date from the latter part of the eighteenth century when, under the influence of the Enlightenment, the strict lecture-system gave way to small seminars, principally in the humanities and theology, the chief purpose of which was the close guidance of students preparing themselves for teaching careers. The seminar more or less as we know it today, however, is primarily a development of the nineteenth century. The names of August Böckh, the philologist at Berlin; Christian Gottlob Heyne, librarian and classical philologist at Göttingen; Leopold von Ranke and Friedrich August Wolf, historian and classical philologist respectively at Berlin, figure prominently. Gradually other disciplines, including law and medicine, adopted the same device. Gradually, also, the program and task of the seminars developed from that of teaching alone to research as well, particularly as an instrument, through seminar papers and discussion, for the guidance of the student in his doctoral study. Parallel with this development was that of special establishments, that is, institutes with specific fields of research activity.

For nearly a century the seminars and institutes operated in the main without book collections of their own, borrowing most of the purely instructional materials they needed from the university library. It became increasingly clear during the last quarter of the nineteenth century that the university libraries, faced with mounting masses of scholarly literature, insufficient staff, the demands of larger student bodies, and lagging financial support, could no longer maintain their role as central, universal book collectors, much less meet the rapidly increasing requirements for materials of the seminars and institutes. Some German university librarians are inclined to argue certain aspects of this statement. A study by Adalbert Roquette, however, incontrovertibly demonstrates the deterioration of the university libraries' financial situation between 1870 and 1892.[25] For, although they all had substantially increased book budgets, varying from 6,450 to 20,100 marks and from 66 percent to 212 percent in capacity to purchase, all but two were 1 percent to 14 percent less well off in 1892 than in 1870 *even if they were to spend their entire funds on the German output alone.* The university libraries were simply in no position to meet new and additional tasks. It had come to be recognized that teaching and research were indivisible; consequently, the demand from the institutes was no longer for small numbers of texts and elementary works, but for a larger and larger volume of monographs, reference tools, journals, and primary materials—in short, for full-fledged research collections.[26] As a result there arose, both from faculty *and* librarians, demands for the establishment of separate institute libraries so that, on the one hand, the needs of the institutes might be met, and, on the other hand, relief might be provided for the university libraries.

It may be asked how the institute libraries could be financed and developed if there were insufficient funds for the university libraries. There are several clear and specific answers. For one thing, the institutes early began the practice of charging their members fees. Thus, an institute with several hundred members, each paying several marks per semester, could count on a steady and substantial book fund. Second, the institutes, as producers of published research, were able to engage in extensive exchanges of both monographic and serial publications with other institutions. Third, many institutes, especially in the sciences and applied fields, were successful in securing direct financial grants, often in large amounts and on a continuing basis, from associations, commercial and industrial interests, and research groups outside the university. Finally, there were regular appropriations from the state to the institutes; from these funds the institute director could spend whatever he wished for books. Such appropriations became a particularly significant factor when the university was attempting to attract a man of high reputation to its faculty. Very frequently the prospective appointee made increased funds for the institute a condition of his acceptance.

The development of the institute libraries, once the movement was fully underway, was extraordinarily rapid. In 1893 Schwenke's *Adressbuch der Deutschen Bibliotheken* listed one hundred and fourteen libraries with holdings totaling 100,000–200,000 volumes. Little more than ten years later, 1904–1905, the figures had grown to three hundred sixty-seven libraries with 616,900 volumes. By 1926–1927 there were one thousand two hundred thirty-two with collections totaling more than 5,000,000 volumes; at the same time the collections of the university libraries contained thirteen and a half million volumes. On the basis of data gathered in connection with this study, the figures for the institute libraries by 1960 were probably at least one thousand three hundred and 8,000,000 volumes.

The growth was not merely in numbers and size, however, but more significantly, in the concept of the institute library as a full-fledged research collection and the place where the intellectual work of the university was carried on. As early as 1906, Naetebus could document the assertion, "There is manifested . . . a development of the institute libraries into complete subject libraries, which no longer stand beside the university libraries, but above them." [27] By the 1930s Hartmann could write, "The age when the university library had the leading position in the collection and administration of scholarly literature for the university . . . is coming to an end." [28] Even stronger was another statement from the same time: "Only today, in an overripe stage, is the problem recognized for its significance not only for scholarly work but also for the university library. For the library, it is a question of life and death." [29] More recently, von Busse has written that the institute libraries "threaten to make the university library obsolete." [30]

From the beginning, the institute libraries were wholly independent of the university library. The expenditure of funds and the selection of books were, and are, entirely by, or under, the direction of the full professor (*Ordinarius*) heading the institute itself. The collections—nonlending—were similarly organized, in so far as they were organized, and controlled, with access limited pretty much to members of the institute, that is, to its faculty and the students in the field. The collections were, and are, built up almost wholly without reference to the university library.

Inevitably these and other conditions gave rise almost from the beginning to grave problems and to serious disagreement and disputation, not to say strife, between the university librarians and the institute directors. The history need not be considered here. Suffice it to say that discussions and memorials at all levels have continued for nearly three quarters of a century; that the problems, more serious now than ever before, are still very far from being resolved; and that the German university librarians have, almost to a man, long been aware of the serious disadvantages of the present situation to the universities, to scholarship, and to the libraries. As one writer noted, "since then [*i.e.*, 1909], we have taken not a single step forward in this pivotal library question; on the contrary, we have traveled many steps further into our fate." [31] The situation as it exists today calls for explication because it bears upon selection policy and collection building.

The *Ordinarius* in charge of a seminar or institute is an all-powerful king in his realm. In it he is, as one librarian characterized him, "more than the dear Lord" (*"mehr als der liebe Gott."*) The *Ordinarius* is, also, very powerful generally in the university. Munich provides dramatic evidence of the might of the institutes and their professor-directors. After World War II, which destroyed much of the University, its Senate voted to appropriate about 85 percent of the Library's quarters to provide space for the institutes and their libraries. It was frankly stated that "though there are certainly many nice books (*schöne Bücher*[!]) in the University Library," the faculty's prime concern and interest were in the institute libraries and their speedy re-establishment at whatever cost. Among the tragic results of this action only two need be mentioned. Fifteen years later, 50 percent of the total book collection still lay unused and unusable in wooden cases. Whereas, before the war, the Library had

600 seats for a student body of 8,000, in 1960 it had 120 seats for 18,000.

Finally, in this connection, it may be noted that book expenditures for the institute libraries frequently equal and sometimes exceed those for the entire university library, with individual institutes often having at their disposal funds ridiculously out of proportion. At Freiburg, as an instance, the appropriation (1960–1961) for the University Library was 280,000 DM ($70,000), and for institute library law books, 80,000 DM ($20,000). One of the very few precise, over-all comparisons publicly available is from Hamburg. The following tabulation gives the data:

Appropriations for Books and Periodicals
(in Deutsche Mark)

Year	Institute Libraries	University Library
1952	209,124	137,855
1953	185,730	165,232
1954	261,252	132,046
Total	656,106 ($164,027)	435,133 ($108,783)

For the three years, therefore, the institute libraries received over 50 percent more money for books and journals than the University Library.[32]

Except in the case of unusually rare or expensive works, there is commonly little and frequently no coordination between book purchases for the institute libraries on the one hand and the university library on the other. Among the many statements on this aspect of the problem which might be adduced here, only one, from the dean of German university librarians, need be cited: "thus it is now high time to bring into one system, through homogenous libraries on the same spot, at least the acquisition of the [scholarly] output, and to treat the book system of a university as a unity."[33]

There is, in fact, little long-range planning or coordination within the institute libraries themselves. This results from three circumstances: the uniquely powerful and autonomous position of the institute director; his concern for building up the library collection to support his particular research interest and specialty; and his often relatively short tenure. As soon as a new director takes office, he sees to the acquiring of materials in *his* specialty and that of his predecessor is ignored. Not infrequently the new institute director cancels periodical subscriptions, often of long standing, so as to be able to subscribe to the specialized journals pertinent to his particular research interest.[34] The situation is such that many of the few faculty members who come to the *Referenten* with book purchase requests, do so, as they are free to admit, because their *Ordinarii*, though generously supplied with book funds, turn them away.

Further, seminar and institute library books, except at Berlin, founded in 1948, are not shown in the university library catalogs. Münster has had, since 1957, a central catalog representing the holdings of some fifteen of the most important institute libraries, and Hamburg's city-wide union catalog, begun in 1945, receives new acquisitions from about a third of some one hundred institute libraries.

It may be noted, without going into detail, that numerous attempts, some of them very early, were made to display total university book resources in a central union catalog. Marburg, for example, in 1845, and again in 1856, when the University had twelve institutes, tried to do so. Despite formal Senate approval and directive, the attempts, like others elsewhere, were abortive.[35] More generally, the Prussian Decree (*Erlass*) of 1891 actually ordered university library-institute cooperation in the building and maintenance of union catalogs.[36] Only Berlin (1892–1897) and Bonn (1892–1899) ever seriously attempted to comply.

In about nine cases out of ten, institute libraries are not cataloged or administered by professional librarians. At Erlangen and at Würzburg, the 50 to 60 institute libraries had, in 1960–1961, not a single professional librarian among them. There were four for Kiel's 90-odd institute libraries, seven for Freiburg's 96, five for Tübingen's 71, twelve for Berlin's 80, three for Saarland's 70, ten and fifteen, respectively for Münster and Hamburg, each of which had approximately 100 institute libraries. A happy development at Hamburg which, it may be hoped, will be intensified there and emulated elsewhere, is represented by a (city) Senate directive requiring that board or agency libraries (*Behördenbüchereien*) of 20,000 or more volumes and institute libraries of 10,000 or more volumes be administered by professional librarians.[37] As a consequence of the prevailing situation there is an almost infinite variation, not simply from university to university, but also from institute to institute within a given university, in every aspect of cataloging and classification, with the result that the researcher's use of an institute library not familiar to him is difficult and time-consuming. As Reincke noted: "Every possible and imaginable variation is represented in the size of cards. . . . the arrangement and extent of entries, the form and number of cross references and the like." [38]

A student who is not a member of a seminar or institute finds it difficult to enter the customarily locked doors. Although lip-service is commonly given to the accessibility of institute libraries to the generality of students, it is universally admitted that such access requires the cutting of considerable red tape, is discouraged, and that nonmember users are not welcome. A frequent explanation, no doubt often with considerable factual justification, is the lack of reading room space. In any case, the decision to admit or exclude rests solely with the institute director and, for all practical purposes, in the hands of the assistant in charge—typically either a young doctoral student working part-time or a high school-level girl, both without any library education. It comes as a considerable shock to the uninitiated to see a chief or assistant university librarian knock on the locked door of a 25,000-volume institute library, only a few steps from his own office and request permission to come in. If the seminar happens not to be open for business, he doesn't get in.

The libraries are almost without exception *Präsenzbibliotheken*, that is, nonlending collections, so there is no question of using materials from one in connection with materials from another. Some institute libraries allow borrowing overnight or weekends, but they are in the minority. Writing indirectly to this point, in connection with a study made at Göttingen, Hartmann noted, "The cases in which use in the institute [library] suffices are quite in the minority; even then, a complicated application for permission from the pertinent director is first necessary." [39]

The institute library as a nonlending establishment was officially recognized as early as 1891. The first of the eight directives of the ministerial decree (*Erlass*) of that date, cited above, declared that the libraries of the university institutes were noncirculating libraries; the books belonging to them were to remain permanently in the institute rooms and, in particular, might not be lent out. For the University of Berlin, the ministry reserved to itself the sole right to make exceptions.

Thus, the picture is that of a main or general library, though one with highly specialized collections in depth, plus numerous independent, completely autonomous libraries each serving a very restricted group of the university community. The grave disadvantages of this scheme of things are obvious. It is wasteful of funds because of the excessive duplication of titles and because those in charge of the libraries do not know the book market. Some university libraries can cite examples of institute libraries buying from dealers' catalogs, for two to three times the published price, in-print books still available from the publisher at the original price. It is not uncommon to find, in or immediately adjacent to the university library, a large institute library, building a collection not simply of the same kinds of materials but buying precisely the same titles as the university library, each often in duplicate copies. The system produces university book resources which are uncoordinated. It makes utterly impossible, as both librarians and professors freely admit, a general, planned collection-building policy for the university as a whole. It creates numerous library empires, some of them very sizeable indeed, of which no university official outside the institutes and seminars themselves, has any real knowledge or control.

A disadvantage of another kind has been the virtual estrangement or alienation of the professor from the university library. This deleterious result began to make itself felt very early, before the end of the nineteenth century, in fact. One report of the period is indicative.

The increase and independent development of the institute libraries had, for the University Library, the disadvantageous result that part of the faculty lost their former, often very keen, direct *personal interest* in the prosperity of the Library. Whereas formerly the Library got as a matter of course all books received from supporting agencies and from private gifts, now, competition of the institute libraries came more and more to be felt; this competition often seriously damaged the Library.[40]

The stronger the institute library became, the more nearly it tended to satisfy all of the faculty man's research needs, with the result that many now have nothing whatever to do with the university library, though they may occasionally send an assistant to it to look up something. The highest estimate obtained, and a lone one, of total faculty personal use was 25 percent. Most estimates were less than 10 percent. Well-appointed, handsome faculty reading rooms, (*Dozenten-Zimmer*) stocked with good collections of reference works, commonly have less than a dozen users, these mostly regulars. The elegant but very small faculty reading-reference room in Bonn's library, completed in 1960, was not made larger because, in the words of the librarian, "it wouldn't be used anyway." The *Jahrbuch der Deutschen Bibliotheken* includes statistics on the "number of borrowing faculty." The figures are seldom as high as a half, and frequently less than a third of total faculty. The great majority of this borrowing is done through assistants, and there is no indication of the number of titles borrowed. Comparable statistics are not generally kept by American libraries, but faculty borrowing and use in most universities are certainly very much greater, perhaps approaching 90 percent. At Columbia, for example, 80 percent of the faculty reported weekly or more frequent use of the library; "the remainder . . . used the Libraries less frequently." [41] Somewhat similarly, at Michigan 89 percent of the faculty use the library once a month or oftener; 77 percent use it several times a month or oftener. [42]

Above all, by making effective use of the total book resources of the university impossible, the present German situation works a disservice to scholarship and learning. For these are not today, nor have they for some time been, composed of compartmented, mutually exclusive segments, each sufficient unto itself. The fields of research cut across one another in an increasing and almost infinite number of ways. The art historian studies the illuminated capitals of a music manuscript; the musicologist frequently turns to history; the historian is dependent upon the economist, whose study of depressions sends him to literature in psychology; the psychologist has need for material in anatomy; the anatomist may be half anthropologist; the anthropologist cannot ignore sociology; the sociologist studies the findings of the archeologist; *his* researches are enormously benefited by the chemist's carbon 14; the chemist may work as much in the field of physics as in his own; the physicist in his study of sound may turn to the musician; and the musician seeks the aid of art history. And thus we close this small circle, one of thousands that could be drawn around and through the branches of the world of learning. The point being one of paramount importance, it may be pursued further by an example in depth. Assume the typical case of a medievalist whose primary interest is with German historical manuscripts from the crusades to the mid-fifteenth century. Such a man must be, almost as much as anything else, a Medieval Latinist. He must also know Middle High and Middle Low German. He will be concerned, from time to time, with Old French and Old Italian. He will be deeply involved with the economic, political, and social events and influences of the period. Questions involving law, theology, and folklore may, on occasion, be of fundamental interest to him. To what fields, in fact, may this scholar not need to turn in his study of the literature? This scholar or, in fact, almost any other. For the notion, sometimes heard, that it is only in work in the humanities and social sciences that collections cutting across several fields need be used, is quite false. As one scientist has noted, "[it was] found that material needed for carrying on research in bacteriology was housed in six different departmental libraries." [43] In the German university much of the most important and specialized material in these many fields will be scattered throughout a dozen or more institute and seminar libraries, their holdings not represented in the catalogs of the university library.

It must be observed, finally, that the role of the faculty in book selection for the university library in all but one of the institutions may be characterized as varying from negligible to virtually nonexistent. The *Deutsche Forschungsgemeinschaft* noted, "during the course of the last decades, many scholars have become so fully accustomed to complete reliance on their institute libraries for their work, that the development of these libraries appears to them much more urgent than does that of the university library from which they have estranged themselves." [44] At Berlin, Bonn, Erlangen,

Frankfurt, Göttingen, Heidelberg, Mainz, Munich, Münster, and Tübingen less than 1 percent up to 3 percent; at Giessen, 5 to 6 percent; and at Marburg up to 25 percent of total book purchases are believed to result from faculty recommendations. Although under no legal or official obligation whatever to do so, the librarians actually buy 90 to 100 percent of the recommended titles. The large number of faculty-recommended titles at Marburg is very likely in part the result of a letter which the librarian writes each new faculty member soliciting information as to his book wishes.[45]

The fault does not lie with the libraries. They make order slips available and most place desiderata books (*Wunschbücher*) in reading rooms. Page after page of these books may be looked through without revealing a request from a faculty member.

The primary reason for the negligible role of the faculty in book selection is, of course, that the institute libraries contain, or can acquire, most of the materials that the faculty need. The very expensive work constitutes a common exception. It is at this point, and generally speaking, only at this point, that the professor comes, hat in hand, to the librarian or *Referent*. He does not usually come in vain. As has been suggested in another connection, the professor should be the library's best customer, its most avid supporter, and its most interested abettor. The role of customer, supporter, and abettor cannot be played without an active concern for the library's book collections. The typical German professor is none of the three.

Although the institute library is administratively, functionally, and bibliothecally isolated from the university library it has, here and there, an informal relationship to the librarians and *Referenten*, particularly where the subject field of librarian and institute are the same. In such cases library staff often are personally acquainted with assistants and professors in the institute. It is also true that, especially among some of the younger *Referenten*, a conscious effort is being made to increase contacts and cooperation with the institute libraries, through consultation with faculty and provision of bibliographical assistance. Some of the institute libraries, in turn, as they have grown large, have turned to the library for help in cataloging and classification and in securing personnel. Such help has been sought and given at Frankfurt, Munich, Würzburg, and elsewhere.

But it is also true that many *Referenten* have never even visited some of the institute libraries in the fields of their responsibility; that they do not, under present conditions, have anything like the time necessary for really effective work with them, even when the institute atmosphere is favorable; that university librarians' offers of cooperation have been repeatedly rebuffed by institute directors; and that, with very few exceptions, the faculty are quite content with the *status quo*. A number of *Referenten* have, in fact, the strong feeling that, though a visit to an institute library would not be taken amiss, regular visits would be definitely resented as unwarranted interference and an attempt to "snoop," supervise, or criticize.

For the first time, apparently, at least in West Germany, there is under active consideration a proposal to establish branch libraries (*Aussenstellen*) under the control of, but outside the walls of, a university library. Göttingen proposes to place such branches in the Otto Hahn Library of the Max Planck Gesellschaft and in the humanities faculty. Books and personnel would be provided by the University Library.

The general willingness of the libraries to assist the institute libraries and to cooperate and coordinate with them is typified by a Freiburg pamphlet, issued with the approval of the Ministry and ratified by the Senate Library Committee.[46] After offering helpful suggestions on acquisitions records, cataloging, etc., the document goes on to note that the University Library regularly sends to the institutes copies of author cards of important new titles acquired, displays such titles in the professors' room (*Dozenten-Zimmer*), issues and distributes lists of them, provides collection depots for order cards, etc. Most of these procedures exist at most other libraries, as well. Most of them have given materials, especially journal files and current subscriptions, to the institutes on permanent or long-term loan. Thus Kiel in 1959–1960 had out on such loans 136 titles—over 3 percent of its total subscriptions—at a cost to the Library of about $2,628.[47] Except, however, as previously noted, for consultation on expensive works and submission of newly acquired journal titles, university library-institute library cooperation is largely a one-way street. Almost without exception institute li-

braries have consistently declined to send regularly to the university
library notices of *their* new acquisitions.

The total German situation is certainly bad for the university library, which, after all, has its *raison d'être* in its service to the
faculty and their students. The faculty is, or should be, the library's
best customers and most ardent supporters. In Germany it is neither.

It might, however, at first glance appear that the situation is ad-
vantageous to the individual German scholar, since he has most of
what he requires close at hand and under his own control. Actually,
the over-all situation is not to his advantage. He does not know, and
can not find out, what the total resources of the university in any
field are. Effective use of the libraries of institutes other than his
own is difficult. Excessive duplication of titles among the institutes
and between them and the central library reduces the number of
individual works which might be available to him. Competition,
especially for gift and exchange material, between the institute
library and the main library cannot work to the advantage of both
and often leads to hard feelings. The independence and isolation
and, it must be said, the prevailing attitude within the institutes,
have generally prevented their libraries from benefiting as much as
they might have from several kinds of professional assistance from
the main library.

The library collections of the German university may be likened
to a great garden which was once open, spacious, and everywhere
accessible to the visitor. The garden is now broken up into numerous
smaller plots. The largest of these—the university library—is still
open and accessible but, relatively speaking, no longer so spacious.
The other plots, enclosed by fences, are neither visible nor readily
accessible to the visitor. No outsider knows what is in them and no
one knows or cares what is being cultivated in the one next door.
The beauty, usefulness, and satisfactions of the garden, as a unified,
planned whole, have been destroyed. Much of the value of the unity
that once existed has been dissipated by the unnecessary duplication
of plantings in different plots, by the fences that exist around them,
and by the almost complete lack of coordination among them.

The preceding strictures are not intended as argument against
the institute library as such. It has unquestionably justified its exist-

ence, just as, in the American university, the divisional, branch, or school [48] library has justified its existence. The argument is against the present administrative and organizational situation, specifically in sum, the lack of a general university book-collection-building plan, of centralization and coordination—in budgeting, book selection and collection building, book purchase, and cataloging—and against the limitations on use.

It might be argued that the German university *does* have a general book-collecting-plan, or policy, namely to support the professors, through the institute libraries, with the books they think they need at hand (regardless of expense or any other consideration) and to provide some of these books and other books to a general university clientele through the university library. It might then be further argued that the resulting expensive duplication and other disadvantages noted are so only from a bibliothecal point of view, not to the happy professor whom policy should make content. Neither argument, however, will bear examination. The growth of the institute library was not a planned development. The growth of individual institute libraries, also, has not been characterized by consistent planning. There is no planned relationship between the development of the institute libraries on the one hand and the development of the university libraries on the other. Much, perhaps a majority, of the total support of the institute libraries has come, not from the universities, but from outside them, and is subject neither to university control nor plan. No one can say whether the total book resources are adequate to the needs of the university because no one knows what is in the aggregate of the institute libraries. And, though the individual professor is generally quite content within his institute library situation, he would be far better served than he is today if total university book resources were developed as a planned unity, if a central catalog were at his disposal, if he could easily use all library book collections, and if some of the present great duplication were diverted to the purchase of additional titles.

The two lessons which history here provides are very clear. A major cause of the development of the wholly independent institute library rests primarily with the university libraries' inability or unwillingness, for whatever cause, to meet the legitimate requirements

of a changing situation. Had they done so—and this is not to say
that the doing would have been easy—the course of German university library history probably would have been vastly different.[49]
The second lesson is that when the library fails to meet strongly felt
needs of its primary customers they are very likely to find a way
toward the fulfillment of those needs outside the framework of the
library's operation and control.

One other observation may be made. Much of the strength and
success of the German university libraries has unquestionably resulted from the fact that they, like most other Continental university libraries such as those of Austria, have been under government control. This independence from the universities has, however,
been bought at the price of a lack of contact with the institution
the library serves. It seems more than likely that this situation was
a contributing factor in the development of the independent institute library. The question has not been critically examined. It appears to be a subject that deserves study.

Other elements probably contributing to the development of the
independent institute library should be noted. Convenience was one
consideration and, of course, a legitimate and important one. The
German university traditionally lacks a campus in the American
sense. The buildings are widely scattered throughout the town or
city, and many institutes are geographically remote from the university library. The factor of status, that is, the library as symbol
in physical form, may have been present. The power and prestige-
conscious *Ordinarii* were often empire-builders, and a large and
important library is a recognized sign of empire in the academic
world. Coupled with this was the quite natural feeling on the part
of the institute director that his freedoms with respect to the library
would be greatly curtailed were it not independent and entirely
under his control. Finally, ignorance of what the university library
would and could do for an institute may sometimes have been a
factor. This seems a rather less likely cause, however, in view of the
fact that the institutes through their earlier days had depended entirely upon the university library, as had also the professors.

It should probably be made clear here that the American situation
is short of the ideal. American campuses still have some independ-

ent libraries, book buying is not always wholly centralized, and there does not everywhere exist a complete union catalog. But in a large majority of American universities most library collections come under a single administration; most book buying is centrally performed, although, as discussed hereafter, book selection is decentralized; a more or less complete union catalog is maintained; and certainly there is a free and untrammeled use of the universities' entire book resources by their faculty and students. (Relatively early examples of various kinds of centralization are, of course, not uncommon. As an instance, Winsor, at Harvard in 1880, was able to institute centralized purchasing and cataloging of all books acquired by any means by any department except the Law School.) [50] What is perhaps equally, or more important, is that a steady progress and a striving toward improvement have been abundantly apparent in recent years, whereas little of the sort is evident on the other side of the Atlantic. Works, in his 1927 study covering eight of the very largest and eight other large university libraries, was able to speak of "a well-defined movement . . . designed to make for a centralization of library service . . . [that is] a movement . . . designed to place the responsibility for handling the library resources in the hands of the librarian." [51] But it was still true at the time that in twenty-five out of forty-eight land-grant colleges and universities separate libraries were administered independently of the central library, and that in fifteen of these institutions books in the separate libraries were not entered in the main library catalog.[52] Ten of the twenty universities reported on in the American Library Association's 1926 *Survey of Libraries in the United States* had from one to twelve separately administered departmental libraries.[53]

The history of the intervening years amply bears out Works's statement. Almost everywhere the number of *independent* book collections has decreased, union catalogs have been improved, centralized purchasing has expanded, and branch libraries have been provided with professional staff. A fairly typical development may be cited in support and by way of illustration. In 1911 the Standing Orders of the Regents of the University of California provided:

Departmental libraries shall be considered part of the working equipment of the departments . . . to be provided in the same manner as other equipment, *viz.*, by purchase with funds allowed the departments in the annual budget. . . . The book funds of the general library shall not be diverted [!] to the purchase of books for departmental libraries. The heads of departments shall have responsible control of the books in their respective departmental libraries. . . .[54]

In 1911 most of the department libraries were small . . . haphazard in content, inadequately housed . . . under little or no supervision and with scant accommodation for readers. Books were bought through the purchasing office on requisition from the departments. . . . Few departments maintained any systematic record of their orders or possessed a list of the books on their shelves.[55]

Subsequently, the library was named the central purchasing agency for all departmental book orders; the holdings of departmental libraries were recorded in the main catalog; adequate supervision of the libraries was provided.[56] Today the Standing Orders read, in part: "All manuscripts, books, periodicals, and maps belonging to the University shall be deposited either in a general or departmental library." [57] This sentence, by itself, could mean little; but, by presidential directive:

As a matter of general policy, all university-owned library facilities connected with each campus shall be respectively under the administrative jurisdiction of the . . . librarians. Proposals to create or continue libraries independent of this administrative jurisdiction will be considered only when exceptional and compelling reasons exist, and shall require the approval of the Chief Local Administrative Officer and the President.

Also, if steps have not already been taken, consideration should be given to the early development of arrangements for coordinating the administration of independent libraries . . . with the campus library system.[58]

To take the Berkeley campus as illustration: All books ordered for official use are centrally purchased and (except for expendable office books) cataloged by the General Library; all of some twenty branch and divisional libraries are professionally staffed, are under central administration, and have their holdings recorded in the main catalog. Two partial exceptions are most music scores and books in Oriental vernaculars, which are cataloged by the East Asiatic Library, a branch library, whose holdings are not included in the central catalog. Numerous other institutions underwent basically similar developments, especially between the 1930s and the 1960s. At Indiana, for instance, in 1942 all of the thirteen branch libraries were put under the central control of a director of libraries.[59]

These examples, pertaining to state universities, may be considered typical. The fundamental concept is found repeatedly and may be cited in two further references to private universities:

> All books, maps, charts, and other printed matter given to the University or purchased from funds appropriated by the Trustees or given for that purpose shall be deemed a part of the Libraries and shall be marked and cataloged as such; and all such purchases shall be made by the Libraries. . . .[60]

> All books, periodicals, pamphlets, maps, manuscripts, and other library materials . . . obtained for University purposes by any library or any other unit of the University through purchase, gift, or exchange or any other means shall form the library collections of the University.
> These collections and their physical facilities and staffs, [with four exceptions] shall constitute the University Library under the direction of the University Librarian. . . .
> Any new library established shall be part of the University Library under the direction of the University Librarian.[61]

Even those once almost universally independent libraries, law and medicine, are gradually being brought fully under the central library administration as, for example, at Chicago, Illinois, and Kansas; the medical libraries are under such administration at, for example, Ohio State and Yale.

Further documentation is presumably not necessary; the reader need only recall the developments of the past fifteen to thirty-five years at Cornell, Michigan, Minnesota, Stanford, and other institutions.[62]

The fundamental difference here, then, between Germany and the United States, is one of broad institutional policy. All large universities have collections of books not geographically part of a main or central library. The library component or collection of books, wherever located, most closely associated with the activity of any university element—institute, department, school, division—tends to be regarded by that element as *the* library. The library is viewed as a specialized service or function of a given institute, department, school, etc., an expression and implementation of its distinctive book needs. This view derives from the natural relationship of man and book. The best policy is the one which makes possible to a maximum degree the closeness of this relationship, consistent with the interests of all—and with the most effective use of university funds. From the point of view of the individual scholar, the ideal would be to have *all* materials that he needs within a matter of feet from his desk, and irremovably so. This is substantially the German and Continental situation, but it is not conducive to the welfare of the whole university, nor is it consistent with the wisest use of university funds. For, as we have observed, collections of books required by individuals and groups are not mutually exclusive, and no university can afford to duplicate indefinitely the materials required by its faculty. The "system" view of American universities, consequently, holds that diverse library elements be coordinated and integrated to avoid costly and unnecessary duplication, to provide total library book resources for the university as a whole, and to make possible maximum effective use of these resources by the entire university community. Part of this view entails the concept of the common pool of bibliographical resources; this concept is almost wholly lacking in the German university.

The position may be summed up and re-emphasized by quoting part of a statement which appears to have applicability and validity for all university libraries.

There is . . . need for . . . a central university library with . . . control over all libraries in the university, or at least coordinating university library services by the appointment of a "Director of Libraries" with recognized authority. Either plan . . . would (a) assure more economical use of financial resources by permitting centralizing acquisition procedures which would preclude the needless duplication of books and expensive periodicals. . . ; (c) afford immediate access to frequently needed material. . . ; and (d) increase the possibility of cooperative acquisition and cataloging among the libraries of various universities.[63]

POLICY AND PRACTICE IN AMERICA

Book-selection policy and practice in America have undergone considerable change during this century and are still in a state of flux. As recently as 1926 the American Library Association *Survey* noted "that, in most of the libraries reporting, practically complete control of departmental allotments is vested in the departments, subject to such centralizing supervision on the part of the library as may be necessary." [64] Such "supervision," however, related almost entirely to matters of duplication, *rara*, very expensive requests, and the like.

About the same time, the *Survey of Land-Grant Colleges and Universities* reported that the only "book selection" activity of the librarians of thirty-three institutions (out of forty-nine reporting) was the avoidance of the purchase of duplicates.[65] The study, which included most of our major state universities, went on to note that "in at least ten institutions library books were ordered by departments without any supervision whatsoever by librarians," and that "supervision by the librarian over selection of books has been considered by some librarians themselves as 'dangerous'." [66] In only five of forty-eight of the institutions did the "librarians . . . exercise supervision (other than to avoid duplication) over recommendations of members of the faculty for purchases from allotted book funds." [67] Thirty-five out of forty-eight of the libraries reported upon in the *Survey* allotted funds departmentally, the funds being "usually considered as the particular perquisites of the departments, to be spent without question as the departments may desire." [68]

Historically, this reliance and passive attitude have frequently, if not commonly, been close to 100 percent. In the early years of this century at Columbia, just to cite one example, the field of Germanic languages and literature was divided into thirteen parts, each assigned to a member of the Germanic department who "shall make himself familiar with the present resources of the Library in the field assigned to him, find out what is most urgently needed, and make recommendations for purchase." The reporter somewhat plaintively continued, "Might it not be well for a representative of each department to visit the periodical room regularly [and] check desirable titles . . . it seems desirable that every department should appoint one member as a library committee." [69]

The situation today is not easily delineated because of the great differences in policy and practice of individual institutions. At one extreme are the libraries for which all of the book selection responsibility and the "free" book funds—money available after provision for journals, serials, reference works, etc., has been made—are placed in faculty hands. At the other end of the scale are libraries—among them some of the largest and best—in which a clearly recognized joint responsibility exists and in which members of the library staff actually perform a great deal of the book selection. Between the two extremes we find a spectrum showing a large number of variations. But in almost no American university is the practical (as contrasted with "legal" or administrative) responsibility for selection *primarily* in the hands of the library.

At or near the first extreme, as one of numerous examples, would be the University of Florida. There, except for the disposition of a few special funds for materials on the history of the State, bibliographies and reference works, the West Indies, and periodical sets, the responsibility and the book money are the faculty's.

There is a tradition of long standing here that the bulk of the selection is done by the faculty. . . . The position of the individual faculty member and his authority to purchase

are not affected by the fact that

many of the recommendations for purchase are originated by the librarians in charge [of the divisional reading rooms] or by the Acquisitions Librarian.

It is significant that the Director of Libraries adds the

"hope that in years to come a certain amount of money will be made available to [him] to be used in [the] general rounding out of the collection.[70]

In the same general category would fall Louisiana State University where

the Faculty is largely responsible for book selection . . . [and] the Library depends upon the expert knowledge and judgment of the Faculty.[71]

The situation is similar at Washington (Seattle) where

Each academic department of instruction is responsible for maintaining the monographic collection in its field and serial publications for a trial period of three years. This is the faculty's responsibility. The librarians' funds are for general studies.[72]

Other characteristic statements are those such as the following:

We expect that each faculty member will order the essential current books and will make inquiry or select from dealers' catalogs the older materials.[73]

The major responsibility for selection of materials [should] remain in the hands of the faculty.[74]

The ultimate responsibility for the selection of subject matter books . . . lies with academic departments . . . 30.7% [of the budgeted] book funds [are] expended by the library and 69.3% [are] expended [by] the instructional departments.[75]

Duke, in 1959–1960, had a total budget for books, periodicals, and binding of $286,000. "Free" funds, after provision for binding, periodicals and serials, reference and bibliographical works, broken files of journals, etc., amounted to $169,000. Of this amount, the law and medical libraries and the academic departments received $109,000.[76] Of California's 1960–1961 book funds, totaling $363,000, about $120,-000 was allocated to general allotments, about $93,000 to departmental allotments, and about $127,000 for current serials.[77] At New Mexico about 88 percent of the total book funds were allocated.[78] Of Cornell's 1961–1962 total book budget of just under $334,000, nearly $172,000 went for journals, binding, bibliographies, and reference works, sets, and microreproduction; about 90 percent of the remaining "free" funds was allocated to subject fields.[79]

Although departmental allocation of a majority of "free" book funds generally means *ultimate* selection authority and responsibility in the hands of the faculty, it does not by any means at the same time imply a lack of library staff activity in the actual selection of materials. At some points at a few institutions the library has come to assume a certain, and often a very considerable amount of specific responsibility. Almost always, however, this is a *de facto* rather than a *de jure* matter; *de jure* the authority remains with the faculty. Where library staff actually act with selection authority, they generally do so with the tolerance and tacit permission of the faculty. Thus, toward the opposite end of the scale range several institutions, among them Cornell, Harvard, Illinois, Michigan, and Minnesota, where the responsibility is a joint one. At Cornell, the entire faculty and library staff is responsible for the upkeep of the library . . . the main work of selection is done by . . . a small number of faculty members designated by their . . . departments . . . the librarians of the departmental libraries, staff committees, the acquisitions librarian, the assistant acquisitions librarian, and the Assistant Director for Technical Services.[80]

The document goes on to describe the responsibility for different subject fields.

Sciences (Physics, Chemistry, Engineering, Zoology): Departmental librarians meet once a week, in Assistant Director for Technical Services' office to discuss their selection.

Art: The librarian of the College of Architecture and the representative of the Art Department meet once a week in the Assistant Director for Technical Services' office. All three bring suggestions and requests and make a joint decision.

Mathematics: Selected by the faculty.

Humanities, Social Sciences (including History, Psychology, and Economics): selected by Assistant Director for Technical Services.

Business and Public Administration: Selected by librarian of Business and Public Administration Library.

The assistant director comments:

I can buy on all subject funds because most of the Cornell departments are willing to let me do the work. However, I have no doubt that any department could at any moment revoke this delegated authority and request that they, alone, order on departmental funds. In such an event, I would not even attempt to fight because I know that I would be licked from the start.[81]

At Minnesota, also, the operation is a joint one, with the library staff performing more than the average amount of selection, the extent of its participation being more or less inversely related to faculty activity.

For example, our history faculty is extremely active in book selection, avidly reading catalogs and reviews and subsequently sending purchase requests to the library.

On the other hand [another department in the humanities] is . . . generally uninterested in building resources. As the chairman of the department once expressed it, "So long as the library acquires the output of the major American university presses, our needs will be satisfied!" Consequently the acquisitions staff continues to develop the library's resources in this area, against the day when a change of faculty or a shift of interests will necessitate having such resources . . .

Most of the departmental libraries recommend purchases in anticipation of faculty needs. . . .

The staff feels it is their right and responsibility to select, but believes that it is their *primary* responsibility to see that *someone* knowledgeable is selecting for each area . . . we have what might be called residual responsibility for developing the library's resources.[82]

At Chicago, likewise,

selection . . . is by both members of the faculty and members of the Library staff. The proportion and activity of these two groups vary from subject field to subject field. In most of the sciences and social sciences, departmental librarians do virtually all of the selection. . . . At the other extreme, in many of the humanistic disciplines, the bulk of the selection is done by members of the faculty, though members of the Library staff participate fairly actively, particularly in the selection of current imprints.[83]

Somewhat similarly, at Illinois:

Responsibility for selection lies with the faculty and the Library staff. The faculty is largely responsible for recommending . . . publications in their . . . fields. The Library must take responsibility for the . . . fields neglected by the faculty, for coordinating the collection as a whole. . . . Final responsibility for selection and coverage will rest with the departmental librarian, although much of the selection will be made by . . . faculty members.[84]

There follows a detailed subject list with departmental library assignments.

At Michigan, a virtually unique four-man Book Selection Department, entirely separate from order and acquisition, has "the responsibility for the coordination of book selection," although

a very large part of [the] . . . selection is done by the faculty . . . the selection officer is permitted to charge against allocations of departments and colleges. . . . *If any department objects . . . we change the charge* to the Director's Fund which is a very substantial amount. In several fields, book selection responsibility is delegated entirely to the librarian of a departmental or divisional library . . . for instance, in engineering, medicine, architecture, and a few other fields. In the few cases where the college or department *wishes to retain the authority* to select the books in its field, the Library Committee of that college or department does the . . . selection. . . . Responsibility, however, for the development of the collections in all fields remains with the Director of the University Library and at any time, if we feel that a library committee is not doing an adequate job, we are free to buy additional materials for that collection out of the Library's general book funds.[85] (italics added)

The situation at Michigan, like that at numerous other institutions, may therefore be partially summarized by saying that, although "appropriations or allocations of library funds are made to units of instruction" and "spending of these funds requires authorization by the faculties concerned, it is the responsibility of the . . . Library . . . to insure that comprehensive collections are developed and maintained." [86]

The library of the State University of Iowa is one of only two or three major libraries where book funds are not allocated to instructional departments, but otherwise its selection policy and practice follow the common pattern.

Apparently the most detailed statement of subject field collecting policy and bibliography checking responsibility is Harvard's. This eighteen-page document, exclusive of appendices, lists by country, language and literature, and subject, the fields of Harvard's collecting interests, the bibliographies and journals regularly checked, and the faculty member(s), and/or library staff member(s) responsible. Thus, as examples, for English and American language and literature,

The American and British national bibliographies, the *Times Literary Supplement,* and the *New York Times Book Review* are checked by [four members of the Library staff] [one of these] also checks the Library of Congress Proofsheets, and [two] check several current reviewing periodicals. Professor —— selects material for the Child Memorial Library and also makes suggestions for the general collection.[87]

Almost as many different variant procedures and policies exist as there are libraries. At Columbia,

all requests for materials to be purchased on library funds must have the approval of [one of six] "Supervising Librarians." . . . In practice, of course, there are a number of subject librarians (about thirty) who initiate orders against funds under their jurisdiction, and whose judgment is rarely questioned by a Supervising Librarian. This review by department head and Supervising Librarian applies to requests originating with the faculty also.

Faculty activity in book selection varies with the subject. All are encouraged to make recommendations, but in practice members of the Library staff initiate most orders (except perhaps for three Departments . . .).

We do allocate most of our book funds by subject, but these accounts are drawn upon by members of the library staff in fulfilling their responsibility for selection, whether self-initiated or by faculty recommendation. Again, there are a few exceptions.[88]

Generalization of universal validity is thus in most respects patently not possible. It seems fair to suggest, however, that the basic situation has changed relatively little since the time of the American Library Association *Survey* of 1926. Of fifty-one institutions (omitting three colleges) there reported on, forty-four, or almost 90 percent, had book funds allocated or divided, either by the administration or the library.[89] Reichmann, basing his report on information from thirty-one universities, noted that a majority of libraries "have the responsibility of filling in gaps in serials and purchasing general reading material." [90] The selection of reference materials is also usually the library's responsibility. Further, a very large majority—probably close to 90 percent—of all institutions divide total book funds into two parts, with something like 70 percent for departmental allocations and 30 percent for the library.[91] The library's funds commonly pay for serial subscriptions and, often, expensive sets, especially those cutting across departmental lines, as well as for the classes of material just noted. One generalization may therefore safely be made: in most of the libraries the selection of the majority of monographic works and the majority of funds for their purchase have been in faculty hands.

The topic of allocation of funds is so inextricably bound to that of the responsibility for selection that it calls for examination. If a substantial proportion of the "free" book funds is allocated to departments of instruction, they are thereby automatically given a measure of authority and responsibility for selection which they inevitably lack if cash is not at their disposal.[92]

The discussion earlier in this chapter showed that no German university library allocates any part of its book funds. Almost all

American libraries do so in amounts ranging from about 25 percent to 70 percent. The two systems are, of course, based upon the two different premises, discussed at the beginning of this chapter, as to where responsibility for book selection lies. Most Continental university libraries follow the German system, including the corps of *Referenten;* most English and Commonwealth university libraries follow a system similar to the American one. "The responsible heads of the teaching departments in the university are the best judges of the value of books in their own subjects." [93] The issue is thus a clear-cut one. As we have seen in Chapter II, it was not always thus and, in fact, until toward the turn of the century, allocation of book funds to departments or faculties was customary in Germany.

What are the disadvantages of the system? The first, and possibly least important, is that no satisfactory formula for the division of funds has ever been devised. In view of the enormous complexity and indeterminability of some of the variables involved, it is highly unlikely that any mathematically provable, and therefore wholly acceptable one, ever can be.[94] Even if one could be, its use would be difficult to defend. The disadvantages and disabilities are as follows:

1. Allocation tends to remove the *responsibility* for book selection from the library, where it administratively, philosophically, and usually legally belongs, and places it on the faculty, who cannot be held responsible or accountable.

2. Practically and generally speaking, faculty members as a group, for a variety of reasons, cannot be relied upon to perform the task of selection regularly, systematically, thoroughly, and objectively.

3. Reliance on faculty selection tends to result in unbalanced, uncoordinated collections and in the purchase of books on a personal-interest basis.

4. Allocation of the book funds reduces the flexibility of the library's acquisition program. The purchase of a large collection, the meeting of a sudden demand for materials in a new program, or the building up of an area of weakness cannot often readily be accomplished when a large proportion of the funds are not at the library's disposal. In most cases, *most* of the funds which are now so avail-

able are required for binding, serials, journals, and essential bibliographical and other reference works.

5. Allocation almost inevitably results in at least some neglect of
overlapping, interstitial, and peripheral area works.

6. Allocation encourages inconsidered ordering, toward the end
of the fiscal year, so as to use up the appropriation and avoid the
possibility of a future reduction.

7. The smaller the total amount of book money available, the
greater the likelihood that departmental allotments may be insufficiently large for the purchase of highly important but very expensive multivolume works.

As offset, there seem to be only two possible advantages. Allocation will help the librarian to withstand pressures from departments
for the purchase of more than what may appear to be a fair share
of material. In theory, at least, allocation, by placing selection responsibility primarily with the faculty, also results in a saving of
library staff time. The advantages do not seem sufficient compensa-
tion for the disadvantages.

Of the basic American system, the core of which is the allocation
of a majority of the "free" book funds to departments of instruction,
and primary reliance upon members of the faculty for the selection
of books, we may say that, in pursuing it, the library has in large
part abdicated from one of its major, if not its most fundamental responsibility and professional task, that of building a sound book
collection. This is no new thesis. It has been expressed before and
since Metcalf wrote, "I have always believed that . . . the most
important single task that any librarian can perform is to build up
the collections in his library." [95] The *ultimate responsibility* for
doing so is almost everywhere implied, and in many universities by
trustee, regental, or presidential directive formally placed upon the
librarian and his staff. Yet, as we have seen, in a large majority of
our universities, the major portion of the book funds, and by far the
greater proportion of "free" funds, resides in the hands of the faculty. Continuing the quotation just cited, Harvard's then Director of
Libraries suggested

that too many of us have been inclined to take a passive attitude in this
regard and that the methods of book selection and the directions in

which the book selection turns are too often determined more or less
haphazardly rather than with what might be called "malice afore-
thought". . . . I have wondered if the chief cause for the relative failure [in building collections] was not the more or less passive attitude already referred to, added to too great reliance on faculty initiative.[96]

The library's role as a book selector has generally been negligible
to nonexistent. But the faculty has no administrative responsibility
in this area; nor can it be held accountable, as individuals or as a
group, for errors of omission or commission with respect to book
selection. The library has and can. Future generations will, indeed
"blame us or praise us [librarians] . . . for what we manage to
save and pass on to them." [97] Or, as Graztl's nice phrase puts it,
"The increase of his library gives the librarian his modest, certainly
anonymous, immortality." [98]

The president whose library becomes subject to criticism directs
this criticism, his queries regarding it, or his punitive action neither
to professors nor to departments, but to the library administration.
And the scholar who looks in vain in his library for an important
work does not, in effect, say to himself, "Damn Professor X; why
didn't he order that book?" The scholar very likely doesn't even
know the name of the supposedly "responsible" Professor X of ten
or twenty or thirty years ago. No, the scholar says to himself, as all
scholars more or less politely have on occasion said, "Damn the library, why didn't it get that book?" And why wasn't the book got?
Lack of funds is always a possible, but seldom at least in the past
half century, the likely reason. It is seldom likely because, except in
the case of a set of really great cost, the library of the kind of institution under discussion here does have sufficient funds for the purchase of the important scholarly publications. The reason for the
nonacquisition of the work is far more likely to be found in one of
these related situations: (1) Professor X, in whose field it lay, was
ill, on leave, derelict in his bibliographical checking, deeply involved in seeing a volume of his own through the press, etc., when
the work appeared; (2) Professor X, whose field, let us say, was
eighteenth century European philosophy, had suddenly left the
university—a fact, be it noted, often not known to the library for
some time thereafter; (3) Professor X had a professional or personal

prejudice against the author of the work in question; or (4) Professor X, though a good man in his special field, had little or no interest beyond it. A classic true-life example, far less uncommon than the halls of academe care openly to admit, is of the philosopher in a major university who firmly and honestly believed that little in post-Kantian philosophy was worth studying or reading. Consequently he ordered almost no philosophy books on the nineteenth or twentieth centuries. Another true instance, also from a major though different university, is that of the political scientist whose specialization was Central Europe. Because he disliked what he knew of German political theory, he consistently refused to buy any books in the German language in his field. More common is the situation we may designate as (4a): Professor X thought the title too specialized, insufficiently specialized, "ephemeral," or not sufficiently pertinent to departmental interests. Obviously, Professor X as an individual is not always to be blamed. But, as every scholar who has worked intensively in any segment of almost any American university library can testify, there is a very strong presumption that the lack of important and needed titles must be laid to the door of Professor X as a type, that is, as a general institutional instrument.

The facts in the foregoing paragraph are known to every American university librarian, and to many faculty members. "They [the faculty at Yale] frankly admitted their inactivity in the selection process because of the time which would be involved in their playing an active part." [99] Metcalf noted,

each professor is busy with teaching and research; even if he is deeply interested in the library, it may not be easy to persuade him to cover publications in his field systematically and continuously. If he is enthusiastic enough to keep at the task, he may expect the library to buy more for him than it should if it is to maintain a fair balance between subjects. He may be chiefly interested in a relatively small subdivision of his general subject, and librarians, even when they realize that a well-rounded collection is not being acquired, find it hard to prevent the overemphasis demanded by specialists.[100]

"Well-rounded" and "overemphasis" are presumably used here, as these and similar concepts (e.g., "balance") are used throughout the present study, in a relative sense. It goes almost without saying that no library will, or should have, equally built up or emphasized collections in all fields because the levels of teaching and research are not the same in all. A number of the considerations mentioned above were pointed out as long ago as the end of the last century by Alfred C. Potter in an article, "The Selection of Books for College Libraries." [101]

The phrase, "it may not be easy to persuade him, [*i.e.*, the faculty member] to cover publications in his field systematically and continuously,"—something of an understatement—points the finger at part of one of the gravest practical disabilities of the present scheme of things. For the various reasons suggested we cannot *rely* on the professor systematically, regularly, and thoroughly to cover the output in his field. The need for such reliance must be assumed *if* book funds and selection authority are placed in faculty hands and *unless* the library has a staff of sufficient size and competence to operate a parallel selection program. The other part of the disability, not thus far observed, may be put in this way. In theory, we could expect the professor to check the reviewing media in his field and the publishers' announcements and second-hand catalogs he receives or which the library sends him. But what about the hundreds of catalogs, often in a single alphabet, covering a score of subjects? What about *Publishers' Weekly* and *British Book News,* to say nothing of *Bibliographie de Belgique, Der Schweizer Buchhandel,* and so on? They cannot effectively be routed to a large number of faculty members, nor will many come regularly to the library to check them. Indeed, the library which waited for even ten faculty members to check a catalog of out-of-print items would find little left by the time its order was received.[102] The disability, then, is that the average professor does not have and cannot be provided with the easy and regular access to all of the bibliographical apparatus necessary for the best performance of the book selection task. It has been shown for the college library that regular checking of this apparatus is a significant factor in the quality of the library's collection, and there is no reason to suppose that the same principle does not hold true for other kinds of libraries.[103]

"The library must take responsibility for the subject fields neglected by the faculty . . ." grants one policy statement.[104] Too often, however, for lack of the necessary staff, organization, or money, the library cannot or does not. "Unless great good fortune comes to us through a faculty appointment, the library is obliged to make provision for selection in the weak areas." [105] "Our feeling here is that we cannot rely upon the faculty to do a systematic and consistent job of book selection. The membership of library committees of departments changes frequently, and new appointees are often in the dark as to policy." [106] "Our present quality of selection varies considerably from department to department and college to college. In many cases, selection is done primarily in response to current demands and current research interests and the people who control funds are not sufficiently concerned with adding stature to the collections." [107]

This statement leads us to what is, possibly, the most serious criticism of present American practice, namely the largely uncoordinated nature of the selection and the resulting collections. There are perhaps few who would go quite so far as the university president who expressed the belief that "the faculty [is the worst] influence on the growth of the library." [108] But the generalization in the continuation of the statement has considerable validity. "In most institutions today the professor considers the development of the library solely in terms of his individual needs. Neither he nor his colleagues plan the future of the library in terms of the institution's needs." [109]

It could hardly fail to be otherwise. The average university professor is usually almost as busy as he thinks he is. He reads or hears of a book or book review; the book is in his field; it sounds interesting; and he orders it. He may now and then find time and opportunity to discuss it with a colleague, or the request may go through a departmental committee or book order officer. But to suppose that there is anything like a regular, general coordination of intradepartmental, to say nothing of interdepartmental book selection is quite unrealistic. The majority of titles in the book stock of the typical American university library are there as the result of scores of thousands of individual, uncoordinated, usually isolated decisions, independently made by hundreds of faculty members.

The frequently cited results of the Waples-Lasswell study are worth repeating in this connection.[110] Of nearly five hundred English, French, and German works in the fields of the social sciences judged by specialists in those fields to be of primary scholarly importance, Harvard held 63 percent, and the universities of Chicago, California, and Michigan, 49, 40, and 31 percent respectively. The New York Public Library, on the other hand, where book selection is, of course, entirely the responsibility of a corps of subject specialist librarians, held 92 percent. For five hundred seventy-three book and journal titles combined, the New York Public Library, Harvard, Chicago, California, and Michigan held 92, 68, 57, 45, and 36 percent respectively. The differences were not the result of disparity of financial means. All of these university libraries obviously had ample funds to buy five hundred important titles; all of them were actually spending more money for publications than was the New York Public Library.[111] The difference lies largely in the chancy nature of almost exclusive reliance upon faculty initiative and industry. As the authors of the study noted, "In terms . . . of the data available, the New York Public Library appears more attentive than the other . . . American libraries to the future needs of American scholars. . . . It pays greater deference to posterity." [112] One might add that, in the same way, the New York Public Library better provided for the present needs of American scholars. Unfortunately the data do not make possible direct comparisons between German and American university libraries.

More recently, the Williams study revealed the generally poor showing of American university libraries in holdings of foreign titles from eight countries.[113] The study further showed the New York Public Library ranking in either 1st, 2d, 3d, or 4th place, for each of the eight countries, in a group which included more than thirty university libraries.

The Library of Congress Cooperative Acquisitions Project clearly showed "the immense gaps that at present exist under haphazard and unplanned methods of library growth . . . [and] some of the lamentable results of our former individualistic policies, imposed upon us for the most part by scholars." [114] The Farmington Plan, for which the Project was almost a preview, produced interinstitutional cooperation and is enormously benefiting American scholarship with respect to the availability of current foreign research materials. But the intrainstitutional policies which resulted in the "immense gaps" remain largely unaltered. As Williams noted, "it would be safe to predict that any jury of librarians who examined [the titles not found in any of the sixty libraries] would find many that, in their opinion, ought to be here." [115]

Yet despite the abundant testimony, despite the evidence of the Waples-Lasswell and Williams studies, and others such as that by Eaton [116] and those at Chicago [116] and Pennsylvania,[116] there exists both administrative and academic resistance to change; the traditional policy and practice persist and, indeed, find defenders in high places. Harvard, spending at the time (1945) about $300,000 annually for books, was able to secure only one of six requested subject-specialist librarian book selectors, and this one for less than the half-time proposed.[117]

On the returns from "A questionnaire . . . sent out to some two hundred department heads and selected members of the faculty . . . [at Florida], the one question on which there was the most unanimous agreement was that the book selection should be done by members of the faculty." [118]

Who selects the books? The faculty mostly, and that is as it should be . . . yet few [!] faculties can boast of a clear-cut acquisitional program, because of the elusive nature of their own scholarly activities. As a result, the . . . program is largely a composite of the individual, sometimes casual choices of many people. It is a profile of immediate faculty interest and that interest is frequently inconsistent and spotty. As faculty members come and go, rich collections accumulated through years of effort are often suddenly forgotten. Appalling gaps are sometimes discovered in other fields. Occasionally hobbies are ridden wildly. Perhaps in the long run we could do no better, but this general lack of planning and continuity is expensive.[119]

In view of the rest of the quotation the logician might question the justification of the first part of the second sentence and doubt the conclusion expressed in the first half of the last one.

Presumably with the *nihil obstat* as well as the *imprimatur* of the American Library Association and the Association of College and

Reference (now Research) Libraries, a committee of the two associations stated:

The policy of book selection by members of the faculty . . . is well established in American . . . universities. Consequently, the great majority of the . . . volumes in our libraries are there because some faculty member asked to have them there. *This has been, and is, sound and sensible practice even though faculty members sometimes lack information about the literature of their fields and knowledge of book selection.*[120] (italics added)

A little later the committee noted, "many faculty members, buying extensively in some narrow specialty, have left behind them accumulations of books that will be little used by anyone else." [121]

After making a persuasive plea for selection by faculty members, a professor added, "There is a disadvantage, and we may as well face the disadvantage, that collections . . . could become moribund. That is to say, when the particular member of the faculty retires, or dies, or leaves to go somewhere else, there may be no one to carry on that particular collection, and for a time it may suffer. That is where the librarian should step in." [122] The librarian also presumably "steps in" *if* the gaps caused by faculty temporary absence for illness or some other cause, indolence, inattention, ignorance, overwork, narrow interest, indifference, or bias are to be filled promptly. But there are four weaknesses of the "step in" theory. In the first place, the library doesn't usually know and would have difficulty discovering when its general *reliance* on faculty selection has thus broken down; when, or if, it does become aware of lacks, the titles may be unobtainable because they are out of print, or the costs of searching and premium prices must be borne. In the second place, the theory presupposes the ever-ready presence on the library staff of a parallel book selection group, having the time and knowledge to do part of the job the faculty is supposed to be doing. In very, very few libraries is the proposition supported by the facts. Thus, as an example, from Michigan:

I suppose, if I were to try to put my finger on our worst book selection problem, it would be the fact that too often it is difficult to persuade faculty to recommend books within their fields of interest but in languages which they themselves do not read. Our Book Selection Department tries to make up for this deficiency, of course, but too often it lacks the subject competence to distinguish qualitatively between such books.[123]

Thirdly, the responsibility, as evidenced especially by the departmental allocation of most of the "free" book funds, resides not with the library but with the faculty. The funds at the exclusive disposal of the library, after costs for continuations, reference books, general reading materials, and expensive sets of multidepartmental interest have been deducted are, in most cases, far too small. Most librarians are aware of this, and are almost unanimously agreed that a large(r) proportion of the book budget should remain free and unallocated.[124]

Finally, the library may be not only financially but also educationally, or philosophically unable to "step in" for the maintenance of a collection in a field now of no interest to anyone on the campus.

A number of years ago when a member of the faculty of a nearby institution moved to this campus, the library of the university from which he came obligingly transferred (for a consideration) a large collection of books the professor considered indispensable to supplement his lectures. Unfortunately, he moved on to greener pastures in a few short years, presumably to an institution already equipped with his prerequisites, and some of this heritage of books has been gathering dust ever since.[125]

An example [of a deadwood collection] is a Lincoln collection that is large and flourishing, but is little used because there are no courses in the Civil War. The library has no strong collection of Civil War material to make this special collection an integral part of the teaching program.[126]

In short, the proposition that the library staff can and will regularly buttress faculty selection and take care of its sins of omission and commission breaks down in theory and largely in practice. Little attention is paid to the sins of omission, and it is the rare professor who has ever had a book order—other than for duplicate copies, and the rare and expensive—questioned.

This section may appropriately end with an observation of different tenor. It is probably universally recognized that many outstandingly useful collections of scholarly import in most university libraries are the result of the devoted labor of knowledgeable, assiduous, faculty book-selectors. Important subject-collections of this kind have been built up in American university libraries throughout most of their history, and in German and other Continental university libraries in an earlier day—before the dominance of the institute library—when faculty participation in book selection for the university library was the rule. Viewed in the aggregate, the importance of these collections to university library strength and university scholarship can scarcely be overemphasized. Indeed, if a majority of faculty members in *all* academic departments had been as ardent, as persistent, and as knowledgeable in building library collections in their fields as that small band of great book collectors, much of what has been said above would not today be true. Certainly the important lacks in university library collections would be far fewer and—assuming availability of the necessary funds—collections would be generally much stronger than they now are. However, in the nature of things, the number of great faculty book-selectors has commonly represented but a small fraction of total faculty. And, as has previously been noted, there is considerable evidence to suggest that the building of great special collections has often been accompanied by the relative neglect of other equally worthy areas and at the sacrifice of the balance which a proper regard for the total teaching and research interests of the institution should make mandatory.

The Beginnings of a New Trend. There is unmistakable evidence, when one reviews the current situation and the history of this century, of a trend not only toward greater library-staff participation in book selection, but also toward greater assumption by the library of over-all responsibility both for selection and for general collection building. Testimony on both counts has been offered earlier in this chapter. Reichmann found that two-thirds of thirty-one libraries had authority to purchase "on all funds without authorization of the subject department." [127] The indicated percentage is undoubtedly much higher than obtains for all American university libraries.

Speaking in general terms, Fussler suggests

the number of faculty members who are both able and willing to carry . . . participation in the actual detailed selection of materials is a diminishing one. Academic promotions seldom grow out of skilled bibliographical services in building research libraries . . . the library staff, rather than the teaching faculty will increasingly carry the burden of implementing the acquisition policy.[128]

Coney has pointed out:

At one time, faculty were ready [to choose the books]. . . . As libraries grow larger, however, the parent university increases in size, complexity, and specialization and the professor, who has been busy enough as teacher and researcher, becomes expert consultant, committeeman, speaker, author, and public relations man. As his library has increased in size and coverage a sense of urgency in the matter of selection has been dissipated by improved local access to materials—to put it bluntly, he has lost interest.[129]

In a very real sense, consequently, larger libraries are being forced to assume the selection role. The development may be quite specifically documented in a more direct way.

Prior to my coming here [*i.e.*, before 1946] Cornell depended to a much greater extent on faculty selection than is now the case. In my judgment the present arrangement assures us of a more thorough and systematic coverage than we could get, by dependence on the faculty.[130]

The librarian of Johns Hopkins wrote:

It is true that a somewhat higher proportion of the selections are made by subject-trained members of the library staff than was true in 1955.[131]

As another instance:

I have been able to persuade the Library Committee to hold down departmental allotments and to establish some large general funds . . . to buy out-of-print books.
    . . . I have told all the professional librarians that it is their responsibility to pay attention to the development of collections in their fields.[132]

Expectation and fulfillment in the realm of increased library-staff selection activity are shown in two statements from Southern Illinois. The first, in 1957, noted:

While we are now allocating half of our book funds to departments, we expect to reduce this ratio as our total book funds are increased.

The second statement, only three years later, reported:

The book budget has been increased from $80,000 to $200,000. . . . We now allocate to the 56 teaching departments approximately 25 percent of the book budget. . . . The bulk of the book funds (approximately 50 percent) are assigned to the four subject librarians. . . . The remaining 25 percent . . . is retained by me . . . for special collections, or for supplementing departmental book budgets.[133]

At California:

We are just beginning, as I see it, to shift over from theoretical reliance on the faculty to prospective primary reliance on staff.[134]

Chicago's librarian wrote:

I think the trend is very clearly toward the staff rather than faculty selection in order to get adequate and uniform coverage.[135]

We are now moving toward a diminishing emphasis on a rigid allocation system and emphasizing the maintenance of the collections as a library function. Departmental authorization of every expenditure against an allocation results in very uneven buying policies and a very serious neglect of interstitial areas, overlapping areas, or peripheral areas. . . . As we get more money we hope that we can move away from this.[136]

When a university's book funds approach the $300,000 level, a new kind of central planning is necessary if the money is to be spent wisely. The older method of leaving the planning entirely in the hands of the departments of the colleges doesn't work well when this much money is available. To meet this need [a member of the Order Department has been] given . . . responsibility for planning the spending of the University's book funds.[137]

As a final illustration:

The Library has traditionally depended on the assistance of the faculty in building its collections, but as its scope of interests has widened, it has become increasingly apparent that the Library should assume more of this responsibility.

The Library is therefore reappraising its facilities and staff, and studying new means for selecting and acquiring books.[138]

Change of the kind suggested in the preceding paragraphs is probably more easily affected when, or as, additional authority is formally placed in the library's hands. At Stanford until 1960 it was provided;

The Committee [on University Libraries] shall annually allocate among schools and departments general University funds . . . budgeted for the purchase of books and periodicals.

The 1960 revision reads:

> The Committee . . . shall be concerned primarily with the strengthen-
> ing of the library resources of the University. It shall advise the Director
> of University Libraries . . . especially on matters relating to the annual
> allocation among schools and departments of general University funds
> . . . for the purchase of books and periodicals.[139]

The role in book selection which the faculty should and can play
is, for any university library, demonstrably an immensely important
one. Faculty *participation* in book selection is the major asset of
current American policy and practice, and it should be greatly
strengthened and increased rather than otherwise. Members of the
faculty will read different books and journals, visit and work in
different libraries, go to different meetings, serve in visiting
capacities at other different institutions, and talk to different colleagues, than will any group of librarians. From these numerous
contacts the interested, persuadable professor who is assured that
his ideas will be welcomed, will inevitably bring valuable suggestions for augmenting the library's holdings—even information,
upon occasion, as to the availability of a whole collection.

The preceding paragraph should make it unmistakably clear that
the evidence and position of this study are not in opposition to
faculty *participation*—to the fullest—in faculty book selection in
all its aspects. Quite the contrary. The evidence is, rather, against
the faculty's ultimate authority and responsibility; against the
largely unrestricted allocation of funds to the faculty; against too-
great reliance on the faculty by the library; and against the uncoordinated collection building, inadvertent imbalances, and other
disadvantages which result to scholarship from these policies.

CHAPTER IV

Modern Book Collections

The discussion in Chapter II brought the account of book collecting and book collections through the third quarter of the nineteenth century. The last chapter considered the development of modern selecting and collecting policy and practice, chiefly since 1900. It is the purpose of the present chapter to trace the growth and development of collections in this century.

By the beginning of the century, as reference to Chapter II, Table 2, and Table 3 shows, several interesting developments may be observed. Before considering them, a word about the nature of the data in Tables 3–6 which follow is in order. The sources of the data, supplied by the libraries, are the best available. Those who have worked with institutional statistics, particularly data involving different countries, will not, however, expect the information of these tables to be completely accurate or precisely comparable. Differences in care and counting methods from institution to institution, from time to time, and from country to country; variations in report years and in purchasing power of money at different times and places; the extent to which a given year is typical or not; and other factors prevent unqualified comparability.

In view of what was said in the preceding chapter, it will come as no surprise that, in one respect, the figures of Tables 3–6 tell for the German universities, not university libraries, an incomplete story. The tables do not include, and cannot include, as the data are generally not available, the holdings of, and expenditures for, the institute libraries. These numbered, in 1900, for all universities, something over 200, with aggregate holdings of around 400,000 volumes. By 1960, the figures were probably at least 1,300 institutes with about 8,000,000 volumes. Yet, though these libraries in some ways parallel branch, divisional, and similar noncentral libraries of the American university, they do not, in the same sense, constitute a part of the total book resources of the universities, nor do they play much of an extrainstitute role. The reasons have already been noted in Chapter III. By contrast, most branch, divisional, etc., libraries in the American university do form a part of total institutional book resources.

A special caveat must be noted on the American libraries' expenditures for 1900 (Table 3)—not previously available in published form. For a number of institutions, the data have been drawn from archival manuscript records. The accuracy of some of these records cannot be absolutely vouched for. Several institutions report their data as approximations or minimum amounts. It is interesting to find that a few universities are quite unable to say how much was spent for books as "late" as 1900. But the concern here is not with whether library X has a thousand or two thousand volumes or dollars more or fewer than library Y. The concern is with the general status and development and the over-all situation of groups of libraries. For this purpose, the data in the tables are satisfactory.

The listings in Tables 3–6 carry no implication, of course, that there were not other major or distinguished American university libraries, or that those were the most distinguished ones; they were simply the largest. On the other hand, although it would be ridiculous to say that a library of 1,300,000 volumes is necessarily "better" than one of 1,000,000 volumes, it is fairly safe to suggest that either of these collections is more useful to more scholars than is a library of 500,000 volumes, provided the quality of book selection has been about the same. Similarly with the library of 2,000,000 volumes compared with that of 1,000,000 or the library of 3,000,000 compared with that of 2,000,000.

It may seem unfair to present simply the largest American libraries. Why not, perhaps, a median group? In defense, two points may be made. The German group, including as it does, in each table, all libraries, shows, of course, the largest and best. The list, therefore, represents the totality of library resources—exclusive of the seminar and institute collections—available to the German universities and their scholars. Further, it would be exceedingly difficult to justify as "typical" or "representative" any median group of American institutions.

The holdings of the German libraries increased from 1875 (Table 2) to 1900 (Table 3) by an annual mean of 5,135 volumes; those of the seventeen American libraries which recur in both Table 2 and Table 3 by an annual mean of 4,720 volumes. The median yearly increases of the two groups were, respectively, 4,279 and 2,800 volumes. The figures are in marked contrast to those for the period 1850–1875 when the German and American mean yearly increases were 3,368 volumes and 1,168 volumes respectively, and the median yearly increases were 2,670 volumes and 823 volumes respectively. During 1875–1900, therefore, the average yearly increase of the German libraries was about 52 percent greater and of the American group about 418 percent greater than in the preceding quarter of a century. On the other hand, though it cannot readily be said what would constitute a strong research collection in 1900, it is highly probable that, despite their great gains, only a small handful at best of the American institutions could be so described. It is even more certain that the majority of American libraries still had, by the turn of the century, wholly inadequate, not to say miserable, collections. A collection of 100,000 volumes in 1900 probably represented less than 1.2 percent of the world output of monographs alone,[1] but only ten American libraries had even this large a collection. Eighteen of the twenty-one German libraries had *twice* this many or more, and none had so few. Without suggesting the equation of size with adequacy, it is nevertheless certain that the libraries of most American universities which had begun doctoral programs by that time were in no position to support either them or faculty research. The fact that such programs were nowhere more than a quarter of a century old is scant justification for the wholly inadequate provision of printed materials which most of the universities were making by 1900. Four American institutions had 300,000 or more volumes (around 3.33 percent of the world output, again leaving journal production out of consideration); whereas, eleven—half of the total group—of German libraries fell in this class. Even so, it is rather surprising to note the relatively small size of some of the German libraries in the lower half of the list

TABLE 3

German University Libraries and the

Library	Volumes	Amount Spent for Books, Periodicals, Binding [a] (in dollars)
Strassburg [b]	810,000	53,960
Heidelberg	580,000	20,900
Göttingen	512,178	51,819
Leipzig [b]	500,000	53,295
Munich	450,000	14,250
Erlangen	388,000	23,750
Tübingen	379,877	29,799
Würzburg	350,000	20,615
Berlin [b]	345,571	38,475
Breslau [b]	345,000	31,349
Jena [b]	300,000	20,620
Bonn	285,000	24,320
Freiburg	270,000	33,725
Giessen	256,984	18,259
Königsberg [b]	250,395	38,641
Kiel	240,000	21,850
Halle [b]	228,000	23,225
Rostock [b]	204,500	18,573
Marburg	192,600	31,078
Greifswald [b]	169,700	31,808
Münster [c]	125,667	12,387
Median	300,000	24,420

Blank spaces indicate data not available.

[a] Reichsmark converted to dollars at the rate (average of 1900–1901) of 1 RM to ninety-five cents.

[b] Universities now in East Germany and Strassburg are included for the sake of comparison and to complete the roster as it stood by 1900.

[c] Münster, abolished in 1818, was not actually re-established as a University until 1902 and the library in 1903. However, its collection had remained intact and a Royal Academy, with some faculties, had existed before this date. The newly constituted University was, therefore, in effect, an absorption and expansion of an existing program and facilities.

[d] The American list has been extended to include, for comparison, institutions which, because of later rapid growth, appear on one or more of Tables 4, 5, and 6. A number of liberal arts college libraries had, as late as 1900, collections substantially larger than some of the universities.

[e] For the first twenty-one libraries.

Largest American University Libraries, 1900

Library	Volumes	Amount Spent for Books, Periodicals, Binding (in dollars)
Harvard	575,000	45,053
Chicago	331,000	18,785
Columbia	311,000	25,314
Yale	310,000	14,675
Cornell	249,634	17,600
Pennsylvania	200,000	6,000
Princeton	150,256	
Michigan	145,460	13,948
Brown	115,000	4,948
Johns Hopkins	100,000	6,000
California	88,000	4,427
Georgetown	85,000	
Lehigh	83,000	2,435
Minnesota	75,000	6,000
Wisconsin	70,000	6,575
Cincinnati	67,769	
Vermont	61,000	
New York	60,000	
Iowa State	58,000	10,201
Illinois	55,000	15,000
Notre Dame	55,000	
Stanford [d]	52,000	
Nebraska [d]	52,000	5,221
Northwestern [d]	45,764	5,050
Washington (St. Louis) [d]	41,000	
Missouri [d]	36,000	
Ohio State [d]	36,000	4,889
Kansas [d]	35,237	
Texas [d]	35,000	2,997
Duke (Trinity) [d]	10,000	1,000
Median	88,000 [e]	10,201 [e]

Source: For the German libraries: *Jahrbuch der Deutschen Bibliotheken* (Leipzig, Harrassowitz, 1902); for American libraries: United States Department of Interior, *Report of the Commissioner of Education* (Washington, D.C., Government Printing Office, 1902) for holdings; figures for expenditures, in some cases approximations only, secured direct from the libraries.

(Table 3). It can hardly be supposed that they were able to support intensive research in many of the universities' disciplines. And, as stated in Chapter III, the day of the large and numerous institute libraries had not yet fully flowered.

A striking contrast between present-day concepts of the nature and responsibility of a university library and its support is apparent when one considers that Mainz and Saarland, building libraries *ab ovo* in 1946 and 1950, respectively, had acquired, in *less than a decade and a half*, larger collections (over 300,000 volumes) than had more than half of the German libraries of 1900; some of these—Freiburg, Greifswald, Giessen, Halle, Kiel, and Marburg for example—had been in existence for two to four and half centuries. The same contrast can be drawn from the recent history of the University of California at Los Angeles and the American libraries of the turn of the century.

That discussion of this kind must be limited to quantitative terms is unfortunate but inevitable. We have no possible means for qualitative evaluation of large collections of books in numerous libraries at an earlier point in history. It is reasonably certain, however, that a "universal" library having 5 percent of the world's print or, for example, 500,000 volumes would, other things being more or less equal, offer more material of more use to more people than a library having only 2.5 percent, or 250,000 volumes.

By 1920 (Table 4) for the first time, the largest American libraries had surpassed in size the largest German ones. Though the statement applies to two institutions only, several others were more or less on a par with their German sisters. Further, the glaring over-all disparity of Table 3 is much less apparent. More important still, the general picture of available book funds greatly favored the American libraries; nineteen (of the first twenty-one) had more than any German one. This is reflected in the average yearly increase per library of the two groups, 1900–1920. The mean and median figures for Germany were 8,856 and 7,250 volumes respectively; for the United States, 15,707 and 12,300 volumes.

Although the median size of the German libraries (486,000 volumes) remained significantly larger than the median (300,000 volumes) of the twenty-three largest American ones, the German median had increased, since 1900, by 62 percent; whereas, the American increase was 340 percent. However, the falling off in size of the next institutions was great. One notes again that many American universities, whose libraries were not large enough to be included in Table 4, and which had been conducting graduate programs for a quarter to nearly a half a century, were far from providing anything like minimal book support for such programs.

Twenty years later, 1940, the situation was that shown in Table 5. Its data are in striking contrast to those of Table 4, and in almost unbelievable contrast to those of Table 3. The mean and median yearly increases of the German group, 1920–1940 have risen to 13,900 and 12,500 volumes respectively; of the American group to 33,450 and 22,500 volumes. The size of the median German library has increased 53 percent; that of the median American library 158 percent since 1920. Five American libraries have now become larger than any German one; twelve were larger than any of the German second division; the smallest of the top twenty-three American libraries was as large as the smallest German one; and the median size of the two groups was equal. Even more striking and more significant is a comparison of book funds. All but one of the largest American libraries were better supported than any of the German ones; thirteen of twenty-three had between two and six and a half times as large budgets as the best supported German library or, if Harvard is omitted, between two and more than four times. The median book budgets of the two groups were $79,000 and $24,000, or a ratio of more than three to one. The American group had become not only much stronger in absolute terms but almost certainly, also, relative to world book production, and its members displayed less glaring disparities. In other words, fewer of the *largest* American libraries were weak in their ability to support modern university programs than had been the case in the past. While the same may be said of the German libraries, the statement applies much less fully, and most were relatively not as much better off.

Far less gratifying for scholarship in American universities at the beginning of World War II was the prospect provided by the twenty-five to possibly fifty university libraries smaller than the

TABLE 4

German University Libraries and the

Library	Volumes (to nearest thousand)	Amount Spent for Books, Periodicals, Binding [a] (in dollars)
Munich	789	8,709
Leipzig [b]	700	15,043
Heidelberg	685	
Jena [b]	685	
Göttingen	678	16,154
Berlin [b]	662	14,729
Erlangen	649	
Tübingen	626	8,921
Hamburg	601	8,620
Giessen	507	
Würzburg	500	
Breslau [b]	486	12,789
Bonn	459	9,924
Frankfurt [c]	433	8,036
Cologne [d]	425	
Königsberg [b]	360	7,980
Kiel	348	6,240
Rostock [b]	329	
Halle [b]	320	9,657
Freiburg	300	
Marburg	283	6,253
Münster	282	11,968
Greifswald [b]	276	5,248
Median	486	8,920

Blank spaces indicate data not available.

[a] Mark converted to dollars at the rate of 12.5 to one dollar. The exchange rate is that of August, 1919. The value of the mark on the international exchange plummeted in succeeding months, but its purchasing power in Germany was less affected.

[b] Universities now in East Germany are included here for the sake of comparison and to complete the roster as it stood in 1920.

[c] Includes the holdings of the City Library and the Senckenberg Library of Science and Medicine, both now under one administration as the City and University Library.

[d] Although re-established only in 1919, several existing libraries, most important, that of the city, immediately were amalgamated with University Library.

[e] The American list has been extended to include, for

Largest American University Libraries, 1920

Library	Volumes (to nearest thousand)	Amount Spent for Books, Periodicals, Binding (in dollars)
Harvard	2,028	90,720
Yale	1,157	29,240
Columbia	761	73,900
Cornell	631	26,119
Chicago	599	51,359
Illinois	550	43,000
Pennsylvania	494	20,190
Princeton	444	26,908
Michigan	432	56,000
California	414	26,612
Stanford	320	29,715
Minnesota	300	43,116
Wisconsin	280	26,661
Brown	258	15,975
Johns Hopkins	226	22,878
Texas	226	41,729
Ohio State	211	21,500
Northwestern	192	10,371
Iowa	185	31,400
Missouri	171	13,000
New York	ca 155	14,976
Nebraska	150	16,500
Kansas	136	18,000
Washington (St. Louis) e	102	11,000
Washington e	96	13,500
Duke (Trinity) e	54	5,500
California (Los Angeles) e	28	3,300
Median	300 f	26,785 f

purposes of comparison, institutions which, because of later rapid growth, appear on Tables 5 or 6.

f For the first twenty-three libraries.

Source: For German libraries: *Jahrbuch der Deutschen Bibliotheken* (Leipzig, Harrassowitz, 1922); for American libraries: Princeton University Library, *College and University Library Statistics, 1919–1920 to 1943–1944* (Princeton, N.J., Princeton University Library, 1947).

TABLE 5

German University Libraries and the

Library	Volumes (to nearest thousand)	Amount Spent for Books, Periodicals, Binding [a] (in dollars)
Berlin [b]	1,293	37,860
Leipzig [b]	1,288	39,985
Frankfurt [c]	1,074	
Munich	1,073	20,675
Göttingen	928	37,703
Cologne	899	31,929
Erlangen	874	15,924
Giessen	789	21,898
Breslau [b]	775	27,191
Marburg	767	27,191
Heidelberg	766	28,630
Jena [b]	745	18,004
Hamburg	707	32,934
Königsberg [b]	679	21,393
Bonn	663	24,337
Tübingen	595	20,462
Freiburg	576	25,368
Kiel	500	23,853
Halle [b]	499	20,307
Münster	490	25,459
Würzburg	456	14,488
Rostock [b]	439	14,795
Greifswald [b]	426	20,820
Median	745	24,095

[a] Reichsmark converted to dollars at the rate (June, 1941) of 2.5 RM to one dollar.

[b] Universities now in East Germany are included for the sake of comparison and to complete the roster as it stood in 1940. However, Strassburg, recovered by France after World War I, but held briefly by Germany, 1940–1944, is omitted.

[c] Included the City Library and the Senckenberg Library of Science and Medicine now, under a single administration, as the City and University Library.

[d] For the first twenty-three libraries.

Largest American University Libraries, 1940

Library	Volumes (to nearest thousand)	Amount Spent for Books, Periodicals, Binding (in dollars)
Harvard	4,160	266,516
Yale	2,956	183,461
Columbia	1,715	198,298
Illinois	1,619	141,923
Chicago	1,301	108,169
Minnesota	1,120	119,144
Michigan	1,098	138,823
California	1,081	113,921
Cornell	1,063	57,470
Princeton	960	67,546
Pennsylvania	934	62,039
Stanford	774	60,041
Texas	640	99,930
Northwestern	638	76,487
Duke	600	119,078
New York	592	79,000
Brown	577	50,819
Johns Hopkins	568	40,031
Ohio State	564	91,030
Wisconsin	485	41,174
Iowa	473	53,203
Washington	458	47,173
Washington (St. Louis)	413	18,110
California (Los Angeles)	356	83,700
Median	774 [d]	79,000 [d]

Source: For German libraries: *Jahrbuch der Deutschen Bibliotheken* (Leipzig, Harrassowitz, 1940). Apparent inconsistencies between the 1920 and 1940 figures cited for certain libraries, for example, Marburg, Tübingen, Würzburg, are to be explained on two grounds: recounts, or more accurate counts, which took place in the 1920s or 1930s, and the fact that, until the earlier date, dissertations were not counted or ten dissertations were counted as one volume. For American libraries: Princeton University Library, *College and University Library Statistics, 1919–1920 to 1943–1944* (Princeton, N.J., Princeton University Library, 1947).

top twenty-three. The 1941 compilation of "College and University Library General and Salary Statistics," published by the American Library Association, presents a fairly representative, though incomplete list.[2] Thirty-nine of the institutions thereon reported themselves universities. Ten of these had library collections of fewer than 200,000 volumes, fourteen fewer than 300,000, and twenty-two, or more than half, fewer than 400,000, that is, less than the smallest of the German libraries. So far as the provision of the materials for research is concerned, it seems fair to say that a majority of American institutions of the time were universities in name only.

Table 6 shows the West German university libraries and the eighteen largest American ones with their size in 1960, their book expenditures as of 1959–1960, and also for the German libraries, their size in 1942, the last year before the destruction of World War II, for which data are available.

General comment was made at the beginning of this chapter on the exclusion from Tables 3-6 of data on the German institute libraries. A note on their present status, with particular reference to Table 6, may be useful here. How numerous the libraries are is seldom precisely known, but at most universities they number at least forty to fifty, at several there are sixty to eighty, and the total in a few of the older and larger insitutions runs to over one hundred. The number for all universities is about 1,300.[3] Even less information is generally available on the libraries' holdings. This much may be said, however: they vary enormously, from a few hundred to over 100,000 volumes; at a majority of universities they *total* over 400,000 volumes; the aggregates range upward to over 1,000,000 volumes; and, in general, they constitute something like 50 to 130 percent of the size of the university library. Munich, better documented than most in this respect, had in 1958 over 120 institute libraries with combined book collections of more than 650,000 volumes. Although these libraries ranged up to 50,000 volumes and there were fifteen of more than 10,000 volumes, the median size was only 3,200. At the time, the University Library contained 770,000 volumes.[4] Hamburg's Library contained (1961) about 850,000 volumes; estimated aggregate holdings of the institute libraries at the same time were 1,100,000 volumes. Because institute library collections duplicate to a large degree those of the university libraries, the sum of the two, for a given institution, would be far from a figure representing *titles* available. The university-institute libraries' duplication of titles appears to be very much greater than duplication between the main library and departmental and branch libraries in the United States. Aggregate expenditures for the institute libraries in most institutions equal or exceed those of the university libraries.

These figures are impressive. Many of the institute and seminar library collections are splendid and their contribution to scholarly work is unquestionably great.[5] Yet the libraries cannot be considered as forming a part of the total general book resources of the universities; they provide almost no extrainstitute service. The reasons have been observed in Chapter III.

The institute tradition remains very much alive, and is as strong as, or stronger than, ever. The Free University of Berlin, founded in 1948, had already established, a dozen years later, about seventy institutes with total book collections of not less than 350,000 volumes. The holdings of the University Library were approximately the same. But it was not begun until 1951, and only then as the result of a Ford Foundation grant.

The development at Saarland is even more striking. The original plan called for a central library with institute libraries subordinate to it; centralized book selection and acquisition; a union catalog; and unified cataloging. After 1955, following a steady increase in the number of German professors, the entire policy was changed. By 1960 the institute libraries had achieved complete independence and no aspects of a centralized system remained.

The data of Table 6 continue and strengthen the trend shown in Table 5, a trend which may be said to have begun sometime between the end of World War I and the mid-1920s. Nine of the American group were now larger than the largest of the German group, and medians for the two were 1,817,000 and 837,000 volumes respectively. The American library with the smallest expenditure for books had financial means close to twice as great as that of

TABLE 6

German University Libraries and the

Library	Volumes [a] (1960) (to nearest thousand)	Volumes [a] (1942)	Amount Spent for Books, Periodicals, Binding [b] (in dollars)
Göttingen	1,757	939	104,962
Heidelberg	1,502	781	77,657
Cologne	1,280	791	112,870
Freiburg	1,250	594	100,626
Tübingen	1,173	601	97,306
Munich	1,129	1,094	31,652
Erlangen	1,105	899	53,228
Marburg	933	788	59,769
Bonn	851	677	123,374
Frankfurt	823	1,236	113,003
Kiel	821	516	62,885
Münster	799	500	83,131
Hamburg	797	727	146,862
Berlin (Free University) [c]	379		51,851
Mainz [c]	376		83,753
Würzburg	363	466	46,028
Saarland [c]	332		112,203
Giessen	263	825	28,045
Median	837		83,442

[a] In order to present statistics as nearly comparable as possible, the figures for the German institutions include dissertations though these are, in Germany, counted separately from other physical units. In line with recommendations of the Association of Research Libraries (CRL, X [October, 1949], 460), most American university libraries, including all of those in the table, report their holdings by physical units and, therefore, include dissertations in their totals.

[b] Deutschmark converted to dollars at the rate of 4DM to one dollar. The amounts include grants, primarily for the purchase of foreign literature, from the *Deutsche Forschungsgemeinschaft*. The institutional apportionment of

Modern Book Collections

Largest American University Libraries, 1960

Library	Volumes (to nearest thousand)	Amount Spent for Books, Periodicals, Binding (in dollars)
Harvard	6,697	903,630
Yale	4,395	855,591
Illinois	3,288	666,924
Columbia	2,876	502,860
Michigan	2,818	532,905
California	2,503	771,070
Cornell	2,116	501,528
Chicago	2,094	348,035
Minnesota	1,968	398,550
Pennsylvania	1,665	351,858
Princeton	1,627	251,849
Stanford	1,592	347,135
California (Los Angeles)	1,464	592,455
Duke	1,435	286,890
Northwestern	1,429	278,150
Wisconsin	1,384	379,159
Ohio State	1,369	350,454
Texas	1,350	987,978
Median	1,817	450,039

the special collecting fields (*Sondersammelgebiete*) is given in *Jahrbuch der Deutschen Bibliotheken* (Wiesbaden, Harrassowitz, 1959), XXXVIII, 342–47.

ᵉ Founded or refounded since 1942.

Source: For German libraries: *Jahrbuch der Deutschen Bibliotheken* (Leipzig, Harrassowitz, 1942, 1959, 1961). Because of differences in the German and American budget and report years, the German data most nearly comparable to the American ones are holdings beginning for 1961; expenditures, April, 1959, to March, 1960. For American libraries: Princeton University Library, "Statistics for College and University Libraries for the Fiscal Year 1959–1960."

the best-supported German library; median book budgets for the two groups were $450,000 and $83,442 respectively, a ratio of more than five to one.

The general book stock disparity of Table 6 would, of course, not be so great as it is were it not for the approximately 4,000,000-volume (West German university libraries') loss of World War II. It would still be great, however—most of the loss having been suffered by Bonn, Frankfurt, Giessen, Hamburg, Kiel, Munich, Münster, and Würzburg, and half of it by Frankfurt, Giessen, and Hamburg. Further, some of the over-all loss has been compensated for by very substantial sums provided since 1949 by the German Research Association (*Deutsche Forschungsgemeinschaft*), just as grants made by its predecessor, the Emergency Association for German Scholarship (*Notgemeinschaft der Deutschen Wissenschaft*), founded 1920, compensated in part for the losses of World War I and the economic catastrophe of the subsequent inflation. In 1960–1961, the West German university libraries received nearly $190,000 for books and journals from the *D.F.G.*[6]

In view of the German losses in World War II, comparisons of German and American average yearly increases, 1940–1960, cannot accurately be made. However, if we omit from consideration the six libraries which suffered most disastrously—Hamburg, Munich, Münster, Frankfurt, Giessen, and Würzburg, the last three of which had, by 1960, still not reached their prewar sizes—, a fairly satisfactory approximation may be obtained. Most of the other libraries lost only a few thousand volumes and some sustained no book losses whatever. The mean and median yearly increases for the period, then, were 23,588 and 26,200 volumes respectively for Germany, and 55,572 and 43,675 volumes for America.

The disparities of Table 6 in terms of materials for scholars, rather than in absolute terms, may not be quite so great as first appears because of the fact that most American libraries, in private as well as state-supported universities, have to provide materials for the three large and expensive fields of architecture, engineering, and mining; in Germany at the research level, these are primarily the province of the *technische Hochschule*. As balance to this fact, however, we need to remember that in the United States medicine, and sometimes agriculture (when present) are frequently distant from the general campus, with library budgets separate from those of the main library, and that the American state university does not cover theology as a formal discipline. In Germany the university library covers these fields as well as law and sometimes forestry.

A more telling, even though still only partial explanation of the size disparity derives from a fundamental difference in collecting level. Put simply, the German library in the main eschews the general reading materials, the introductory work, the beginner's volume, which go to make up a large amount of the American libraries' acquisitions. There are two related reasons for this collecting policy, both logically derived from the functions of the German university. Its students are admitted after completion of the *gymnasium*, that is, at about the level of the American junior year of college. The needs of the American "lower-division" student are, therefore, largely nonexistent. To be sure, it is true today that many matriculants are not in a doctoral program and enroll without any intention of working for the degree. Such students come to prepare themselves for teaching positions in schools, for posts in industry and business, and for the state examinations in these and other fields. Since World War II, also, several universities have instituted Master's (*Magister*) programs, in duration and purpose not unlike those of American universities. But the "typical" student is still the potential doctoral candidate, and the university is chiefly geared to him and his needs. In any case all students are, in terms of the German educational system, graduate students. For a century and a half and more, therefore, the German university library has considered itself not simply *primarily*, but almost *exclusively* an institution serving research needs and purposes. Consequently, as considered in detail in Chapter III, the title which is believed not to have present or potential scholarly value, no matter how high its quality, is seldom purchased. Further, the German university library buys almost no duplicate copies; these constitute a not inconsiderable number of the acquisitions of American libraries, chiefly for the required and collateral reading of lower division students and for browsing and general reading collections.

Some libraries, among them Bonn, the first, in 1919, influenced by American example, Cologne, Frankfurt, Göttingen, Heidelberg, Freiburg, and Münster, have established, mostly since World War II, small "teaching libraries" (*Lehrbüchereien*) or "student libraries" (*Studentenbüchereien*) containing multiple copies of much-used course texts and/or general reading materials.[7] These collections are somewhat akin to the American reserve book and/or browsing room collection, but much smaller, usually not over 3,000 volumes.

There can be no quarrel with the limited collecting philosophy, just noted, which is clearly based on institutional function and estimated need. One can only suggest that, as the curriculum of the *gymnasium* is, like that of the United States high school, necessarily limited, and as the German student frequently comes to the university with a somewhat parochial background, the university library would broaden its sphere of influence and further the general cultural level of students if it were to provide more of the "general reading" materials so common in the American university library. Under present conditions of financial support the German library could not do so, however, without seriously impairing other activities. As Luther notes, "Now, as in the past, German scholarly libraries decline to serve recreation." "The European university library generally feels incompetent in the field of leisurely reading. Aside from this, the library lacks the material resources for a setup of this kind."[8]

A much more fundamental question is the one which asks, "What constitutes research materials?" Generally speaking, the German librarian seems surer of his decisions here than does his American counterpart. In any case, he unquestionably selects and collects on the basis of a narrower concept of "research" materials. This obviously results, on the average, in smaller collections. The nature of research materials and their relationship to selection policy are considered in detail in the following chapter.

The greatest single cause, however, of the relatively much more rapid growth in recent years of the American libraries has been their far greater book budgets. Money is perhaps a distasteful word, yet in this case it is the indispensable straw without which the necessary bricks cannot be made. Neither the most successful promotion efforts for securing gifts of books nor the most widely extended program of exchange can substitute for a large (and regular) budget. The disproportionately large sums devoted to building up institute libraries, and the excessive duplication of materials in them, account in great measure for the relatively small book budgets of the university libraries. For the period since shortly after World War I, the purchasing power of the top group of American libraries has been increasingly greater than that of their German sister institutions. The significance is clear: other things being more or less equal, a library with two or three or four or five times as much money to spend as another will be able to buy more books and will, over a period of time, be able to build up a substantially larger collection. Such a collection will, in all likelihood, be of more value to more scholars for more purposes. Reference to the previous tables, especially Tables 1–4, will show how, within the American groups, libraries once ranking high have later fallen behind. It is sometimes held to be almost indecent to speak of a library in terms of its size. The fact is, however, that granted even reasonably good book selection, the size of a scholarly library provides a very fair, even though rough index of the degree of probability that a desired publication will be found in it. And the book budget, equating in large measure to new titles acquired, is a statistic of parallel significance.

It follows from the German-American disparities in these two closely related respects that the quality of book selection per se cannot in the present instance be judged by what is or is not in the collections, since the factor of available funds plays such a dominant and determining role.

Another fact, already mentioned, which prohibits such a judgment is the 4,000,000 volume university library loss of World War II, a loss which, in numerous libraries, included not only bound volumes (and dissertations, manuscripts, and so on), but also catalogs, as for instance at Bonn, Giessen, Hamburg, Munich, Münster, and Würzburg.

Although this study is not specifically concerned with book funds, their relationship to book selection and book collections makes it necessary to point out that almost none of the German libraries has been sufficiently well supported. Granted that no university library ever has "enough" book money, and that size of book funds is partly a relative matter, in which many variables play a role, it is still true that some minimal level of support is essential if a library is to meet the demands which a real university places upon it. With few if any exceptions such support has not been made available in Germany. This is not a subjective judgment. It is supported by repeated observation of lacking contemporary, that is, post-World War I and II, scholarly works, chiefly foreign, and by the constant comments of German university library personnel.[9] It is also supported by a study of the *Notgemeinschaft der Deutschen Wissenschaft* and a memorial of its successor, the *Deutsche Forschungsgemeinschaft.*[10] Even Scheibert's proposed "normal current book budget" (*laufender Normalanschaffungsetat*) of 170,300 DM ($42,575) [11]—absurdly low, as Luther's critique made abundantly clear [12]—had still not been attained a decade later by some libraries, and had only just been reached by others. In the years since the proposal, as numerous studies show, book and periodical production substantially increased and book, periodical, and binding costs increased by at least 50 percent.[13]

This general, and generally gross inadequacy of book funds, is of such vital significance that some further comment seems called for. Roquette, in two careful studies, pointed out, among other things, the relative deterioration of university library book budgets at the turn of the century compared with those of 1870 and 1880.[14] Roquette's estimate, 57,000 M, (about $55,000) of needed book funds was not met by a *single* university library in 1900.[15]

Later, Leyh, largely confirming Roquette's findings and bringing them down to 1922, demonstrated on the basis of then-current book, periodical, and binding costs, a budget of 294,989 M (about $23,600) for 1920.[16] No library at the time had this much and only five had as much as half the amount.[17] In terms of purchasing power for scholarly German works alone, Leyh estimated deficiencies of 12 to 47 percent for the libraries in 1900 and, except for Leipzig, 20 to 35 percent in 1922.[18] Forty years later less than a third of the libraries had book budgets as large as Leyh's estimate.

What had happened in the meantime to world book and journal production and to costs need not be detailed.

Perhaps no other library was forced by financial stringency, as was Erlangen, to the drastic expediency of consciously curtailing purchases for certain long and well-established disciplines.[19] But most other libraries found it necessary to buy smaller percentages of the world output of book and periodical literature.

The over-all picture may be examined in another way, by considering the average yearly rate of increase of the libraries, 1920 (Table 4) to 1960 (Table 6). After eliminating from the German group libraries which appear on only one of the tables and those which suffered significant loss in World War II, seven institutions remain. These include, however, the five largest as of 1960. The range of average yearly rate of growth of the seven is from 1.4 to 3.6 percent, the median being 2.4 percent. For the sixteen largest American libraries which appear on both Tables 4 and 6, the range is from 3.0 to 5.1 percent with a median of 4.1 percent. As the concept "average yearly rate of growth" here is exactly the same as that of compound interest, it requires only a small percentage difference, over a forty year period, to result in a large difference in growth of collections in absolute terms.[20] The American library with the smallest average yearly rate of growth approaches the German library with the largest rate. Every American library shows a larger growth rate than all but one of the German institutions.

In sum, a great deal of conclusive evidence is at hand to substantiate the claim that the support of the German university libraries in this century has been not simply inadequate but, in relation to world book and journal production and costs, has, for most institutions, deteriorated.

No comparable studies have been made for the United States but, though nothing in the foregoing is intended to imply that book funds for its university libraries have been adequate, it is at least clear that for more than a quarter of a century most of the major ones have been far better off than their German sister institutions. Indeed, only five of the forty-two libraries on the

"Princeton" list of 1959–1960 spent less for books than did the best-supported German library; if we except this single institution, only two American libraries had smaller budgets than any German one. The total and individual disparities are very great, even taking into account the fact that binding costs in Germany are considerably lower than in the United States.

There is, of course, a large number of American university libraries much less well off than those in Table 6. However, of the one hundred nineteen institutions which, under a liberal definition, might be classified as universities, fifty-five, or 46 percent, provided greater support for books, etc., than the *best-supported* German library; only *one* of the one hundred nineteen had a smaller book budget than that of the lowest German library. Ninety-six, or 80 percent, of the one hundred nineteen had holdings larger than that of the smallest German library.[21]

The average yearly increases in holdings of the two groups by period since 1850 are shown in Table 7. In about a century

TABLE 7

Yearly Increases of Volumes in German and American University Libraries, 1850–1960

Period	German		American	
	Mean	Median	Mean	Median
1850–1875	3,368	2,670	1,168	823
1875–1900	5,135	4,279	4,720	2,800
1900–1920	8,856	7,250	5,707	2,300
1920–1940	13,902	12,500	33,450	22,500
1940–1960	23,588	26,200	55,572	43,675

the mean and median yearly additions of the German libraries increased seven and ten times respectively; those of the American libraries about fifty times. The American figure is, of course, the average increase from "all" libraries (1850–1875) to the largest (1940–1960) only.

CHAPTER V

What Should Be Collected?

As has previously been suggested, the answer to this question is exceedingly simple. The university library should acquire those materials which, now and in the future, will best serve the objectives of the university, that is, fulfill the instructional and research needs of its faculty and students. For reasons already noted, the answer to the question which naturally follows: What are those materials? is extraordinarily difficult and complex. As has also been pointed out, it is, for a number of reasons, the more esoteric, the more unusual, and the more specialized materials of research which make up the hard core of the problem.

The fact that all true university libraries are intensively and extensively concerned with the acquisition of research materials presumably need not be documented here. Specific reference to the obligation appears in virtually every existing policy statement and in countless reports, directives, and articles. What do, perhaps, need discussion are two closely related points: (a) the German libraries' virtual restriction of their selection and acquisition to this type of material and (b) their substantially more limited view of its nature.

As we have seen in earlier chapters, the policy expressed in the first of these two points was fully formulated in the nineteenth century and has continued substantially unchanged. It is so universally accepted, and considered so self-evidently proper in Germany, that it has in recent years very seldom been a subject of discussion. The reference in Chapter II to the Erlangen rules of 1826 very well represents, in its basic elements, the German position today. Over and over one hears the comments: "We want *only* research material," ("*Nur Forschungsmaterial wollen wir haben,*") or (to *Referenten*) "You must always restrict yourselves to just the most important research material." (*"Sie müssen sich immer nur auf das wichtigste Forschungsmaterial beschränken"*). The intent applies equally, as in the Erlangen document, to gifts and exchanges, as well as to purchases. The same fundamental principle is expressed in a statement on the Kiel Library: "As the name of the Library says, it is *primarily intended for the scholarly needs of the University*. . . . Consequently, the Library cultivates scholarly literature." [1] And it is also expressed at Hamburg: "The Library acquires material of *scholarly importance* in all fields . . . and in addition general instructional writing, in all fields, *in so far as it has a scholarly foundation*." [2] (italics added)

The second point, (b), suggests that the German librarian has a substantially narrower concept than his American colleague, of what constitutes research material. Perhaps for this reason, he also has greater assurance as to what belongs in his collecting policy.

The lack of assurance among American librarians on this point was elaborated by Talmadge on the basis of the Farmington Plan Survey.

First [facet of the Plan] is the one that permeates [it] and causes most complaints. This is the lack of any definition of the phrase "research value" or of "scholarly utility," to guide the dealers. We now doubt that any two librarians could reach complete agreement on a general, working definition of "research interest" if they sat down to work one out. This . . . was tested back in 1952, when four well-known librarians set out to check in the Swiss national bibliography for 1949 the items they thought would meet the definition. Excluding fiction, drama, and poetry, they reviewed 1,022 items. They agreed unanimously on only 110 items, they voted three to one (either for or against) on 396, and on 516 items, just over half of the total, two voted yes and two voted no.

The situation has not changed. What one library calls junk, and complains that the agent should not have sent, another library pronounces of fundamental research value. There are dozens of examples. Here is one: local histories and guide books. One library with an allocation in history will protest that it certainly does not want to go that deep . . . while another library will say, "We are eager to get our hands on anything that illustrates local architecture and sculpture in the country." They are talking about the same books. Please do not conclude that the first library is being selfish and looking only to its own local interests; these people honestly believe that these books are not worth having, even in a single copy, anywhere in the country. Another example is *belles-lettres*, which constitute an especially clean-cut problem, with one institution wanting only first-class authors, another wanting virtually all minor authors in addition.

Librarians are growling—or tearing their hair—because in their opinion the agent sent 25 per cent junk last year, or he failed to send 30 per cent of the significant publications of his country.[3]

The German librarian appears to be beset by no such doubts and differences of opinion. Speaking in very broad terms, and subject to the ordinary limitations and exceptions of such terms, the German library limits its collecting for research to manuscripts; the scholarly monograph and journal; official sources—international, national, state, and local reports—and, of course, the usual transactions and proceedings, handbooks, biographical, bibliographical, and other reference works. What is, in general, conspicuously absent, is a vast body of literature—using the word in its broadest, rather than narrow sense—not belonging to any of these categories, which the following discussion attempts to characterize.

THE NATURE OF RESEARCH MATERIAL

For a wholly adequate foundation on which to base a research-material selecting and collecting policy, we should need comprehensive and widely representative data on how scholars in all fields actually work and what materials they need and use. Unfortunately, we do not know nearly as much as we should about either point. What we do know is chiefly British and American in origin. The studies by Bradford, Gross and Gross, McAnally, and Stevens, among others, are strongly suggestive at the very least.[4] They tend, directly or indirectly, to show that (1) the scholarly library more fully satisfies the literature needs of the researcher in science and technology than the needs of workers in other fields; (2) in all fields, but especially in the nonscientific ones, many references, that is, "scholarly needs," are to one- or two-time cited studies, that is, are to works very infrequently used by the scholars; and (3) in the nonscientific fields, a large *majority* of titles referred to is cited very infrequently. Stevens noted that, of 6,352 titles cited in just "40 dissertations classified as using the historical method . . . 81 percent . . . were titles cited by only one dissertation . . ." [5] It was also true, that "52 percent of those used in experimental dissertations were cited by only one dissertation." [6] These are large percentages, and strongly suggest that the research library which adequately supports its scholars cannot limit itself simply to the obvious, the standard, the basic, and the very important. The studies by Fussler and Waples showing, respectively, the astonishing number of "nonchemistry" and "nonphysics" titles used by chemists and physicists, and the wide-ranging needs of Belgian researchers, also point in the same general direction. [7]

The direct testimony of scholars, though it is not voluminous, is highly illuminating and of a remarkable near-unanimity.

A newly published comprehensive study tends to supersede and make obsolete the older ones on the same subject but a new monograph does not have quite the same effect. It fills the interstices between other studies, or it corrects certain parts of older works, leaving other parts to stand unchallenged. This piecemeal way of advancing knowledge makes it necessary for the scholar to have at hand the whole range of monographic literature, not just the selected best of it. . . . In research libraries, consequently, the ideal of a well-selected collection of books had to give way to the ideal of virtual completeness. [8]

More than this, the scholar, as another of them has written, is

actively interested not only in the traditional account of political and military matters, not only in economic and political institutions . . . [but also in] what men have worn, what they have eaten, what amusements they had, what went on in their heads and hearts. This interest is not confined to the activities of the great men and women who were once almost the sole subject of history; it extends to the activities of all kinds of human beings. Therefore, the scholar will not like it if you find that dime novels, *Buffalo Bill, Godey's Lady's Book*, old Sears Roebuck catalogs, out-of-date textbooks, and such material are an indecent cluttering of your shelves. They want all this, and, being scholars, more too. [9]

Much the same thought is expressed by another scholar who, speaking for his brotherhood, notes, "The scholar needs not only what Arnold called 'the best that has been known and said,' but the commonplace as well, for the mediocre is often quite as valuable as the great in providing an understanding of the climate of opinion out of which grew—or against which rebelled—a Milton, a Molière, or a Goethe." [10]

It would appear that the question with which we are faced is not so much, What is the nature of research materials? but, rather, What kinds of materials for the research worker? The two questions do not equate to the same thing. For it appears, also, that in the nonscientific, nontechnological fields, at least, the scholar, or the American scholar, at any rate, needs, to *produce* modern research, an almost infinite number and variety of literature—*vide Godey's Lady's Book* and the Sears Roebuck catalogs—which does not, itself, in any way classify as "research." Some years ago, Bishop wrote

in certain subjects of study, such as philosophy and social history, practically everything which has ever made its appearance in print may be held to be the expression of human thought and hence of possible importance to research. Researchers engaged on the history of human knowledge . . . those who are concerned with the evolution and spread of ideas, cannot wholly ignore *any* book or printed paper. . . . From the point of view of a student of our civilization there is no limit to the books he would like to have available.[11]

Based on the comprehensive study of the Columbia University libraries, Tauber more recently noted that, in the opinion of faculty, as well as students and library staff,

there is no predictable upper limit to Columbia's library requirements. Almost any journal, monograph, document, or manuscript has (or is thought by someone to have) an actual or potential use in the pursuit of knowledge in the modern university. Furthermore, even though Columbia's present library resources [2,876,815 volumes] are impressive, they fall considerably short of what members of the faculties and library staff consider necessary or desirable. This is attested by repeated references to reliance on other libraries . . . and by recurring references to the need for better coverage of current literature, for acquisition of basic materials in fields of expanding interest.[12]

Because of the German libraries' long tradition of collecting only research material, the kinds of material suggested in the quotations from Bestor, Bishop, Brinton, and Hart do not commonly find a place in the German university library. They also do not find a place in the institute library.

Perhaps the German librarian is justified both in his position and his assurance, but his narrower concept of "research" material at least raises the possibility of doubt. As has been observed, especially in Chapter I, certain classes of material, such as, for example, the original contribution to knowledge, the new interpretation, and primary sources of many kinds clearly belong in the "research" class. Just as clearly, the introductory grammar or mathematics text, or the biography or travel book, restating for popular consumption what is already more authoritatively available elsewhere, does not. But there is a large body of literature between these two extremes. The ostensible juvenile may be a first compilation of Chinese folk tales—and many have become literary classics or sources for major studies: McGuffey's readers, *Alice in Wonderland*, *Gulliver's Travels*, the work of the Grimm brothers. As a small point in fact, *Godey's Lady's Book* is not listed as being held by any German university library. Perhaps even more indicative of general collecting policy is the fact that none maintains a file of the *Readers' Guide to Periodical Literature*.

The case for "unimportant" materials has been put thus by one scholar:

> By any sound standard of interpretation, the great are, in large part at least, products of their time and environment. All are affected, not only by their immediate associates, but by public opinion and popular movements—by contacts with individuals out of the mass of men.
>
> More and more historians and historically minded people are impressed with the significance of social history—the portrayal of the life and thought . . . of the people as a whole. In that life and thought can be found a far clearer explanation of the past than is to be gathered from the lives and thoughts of the great. If this be so . . . then such records as can be saved, which portray that life and thought, are incalculably valuable in the cause of history.
>
> The run-of-the-mine stuff . . . deals with matters about which, often, no other information can be found.[13]

Although the author was speaking specifically of manuscript material, the argument has almost equal force for other kinds of records.

What about the masses of print which appeared in Germany under the Nazi regime, which some German university librarians, at least, brush aside as trash, and will not have in their libraries? As literature, the novels of this period are mostly worthless, but to the social historian they are of enormous interest. So, too, are the nonliterary products of this time to the psychologist, particularly the researcher in mass behavior and to the student of content analysis, propaganda, and communication. Indeed, can the worker in any social or humanistic field write of Germany from the mid-1920s to the mid-1940s without closely examining the Nazi-dominated "cultural" output? A close parallel, even though on a smaller and less extreme scale, is the writing that appeared in the United States during the McCarthy era. In short, what about all the wealth of print which, in one way or another, reflects the life, the spirit, the temper, the creativity—good, bad, or indifferent —of individuals and groups of men?

A more likely explanation than his own purely administrative or bibliothecal decision for the German librarian's generally restricted view may lie in his compatriot's research interests. The hypothesis here is that the German library may have collected more narrowly than the American because the German scholar has, in the main, not demanded that the library provide him with the kind of human record we have discussed.

This is not the place to attempt a critique of German scholarship in the *Geisteswissenschaften*. The views of a German writer on the point may, however, be cited. At the conclusion of a keenly perceptive article, von Rantzau suggests,

Liberal agitations and movements do not flourish within the confines of the government services, they grow upon the soil of social groups and their varied activities. The charge that German political historians have long pushed society into the background behind the state, that they prefer to portray the deeds of military men and state officials rather than the workings of sociological groups, is still to the point. Of course, the advice we are now getting, especially from America, to concern ourselves with sociology, may often ring wearily in our ears. But it is not just a crotchet. It arises because German university scholarship, with its tradition of regarding the study of state documents as the alpha and omega of history, has incontrovertibly entered a blind alley. We see again, in the work of Toynbee, who began his researches as a political historian and certainly does not fail to recognize the historically creative importance of the state, that the introduction of sociological and religious-psychological processes opens wide the historian's horizon.

German historiography must expand the range of its investigations. . . . Among our scholars in the field of history . . . only a few show an inclination and capacity . . . to understand political happenings upon the basis of broader relationships.[14]

COMPREHENSIVENESS VERSUS SELECTIVITY

The considerations thus far discussed in this chapter lead inevitably to the topic of this section and are, indeed, an inseparable part of it. The topic has, in this century, increasingly received the attention of librarians, and others, as the costs of acquiring, processing, housing, maintaining, and servicing the materials for major scholarly libraries have grown larger and larger. Since we concede that no library can hope to collect every existing document, or even every important existing item, on all subjects, the question should probably be rephrased, What kind of selectivity? And yet, granting the rephrasing and despite cooperative acquisition and storage, a Farmington Plan, or a program of the *Deutsche Forschungsgemeinschaft* and other devices which tend to slow the growth rate of individual libraries, an indisputable fact remains. It is that, in those fields, usually numerous, in which a university supports doctoral study and expects significant faculty research, the attempt toward comprehensiveness has existed, persists today, and, under existing conditions, is inescapable in the future. Consequently, we need to distinguish between comprehensiveness, that is, the most extensive and intensive collection, in *all* fields, which no library can hope to maintain, and comprehensiveness *within* certain fields or subjects. The aim toward comprehensiveness does not, therefore, mean that the library of every university offering the doctorate in European history will, or needs to attempt to acquire, everything of importance from or about a relatively minor area such as Yugoslavia. Nor, certainly, does it mean indiscriminate, pack-rat collection which seeks to acquire and preserve every scrap of written or printed matter ever produced. The library's obligation to select qualitatively is never absent. But it does mean that the library will be forced by demands from without itself to try to acquire as much as it possibly can of the useful or potentially useful material on many other countries and periods, including, but not limited to those which have been significant for the development of the Western world. Specifically, it means that in those fields in which the teaching and research program of the university dictate real library strength, the library's aim and ideal will be comprehensiveness. A selection policy which says otherwise is unrealistic. Can there be imagined the library of a university priding itself on a *major* research program in psychology declining to attempt to acquire *any* important materials in this field? The question answers itself. When the literature of such a subject is added to those for all the other primary areas—and many, such as Africa, which would not have been collected a quarter of a century ago—the result is a big open-ended, constantly increasing collection.

Thus the teaching and research program of a given university enables its library to say that, for the field of Scandinavian literature or Oriental art or Latin American history, a good working collection only, with the necessary reference and bibliographic tools, will be maintained. No more than this. We turn aside from opportunities to acquire Bjørnson manuscripts and Ibsen first editions, rubbings from T'ang Dynasty tombstones, Bolivar letters, and so on. In this way and to this extent every library collects selectively. But in the subjects in which the university aims for true research distinction, the library does not and cannot collect selectively—though it still collects *qualitatively*—except as its budget requires it to do so. The ideal in these fields is comprehensiveness.

What we have, then, may be put into graphic terms if we visualize a box, ABCDEFGH, such as that in Figure 1, four of whose six sides, AFGB, EDCH, ADEF, FGHE, have indefinite termini. The series of vertical lines a-b, c-d, etc., compartments the box into the fields of knowledge; taken together, these fields are responsible for the total human written record. A series of lines, a'-b', c'-d', etc. represent chronological or geographical subdivisions, such as history of the Middle Ages, twentieth century art, English history, or Italian art. Finally, suppose a series of four horizontal lines

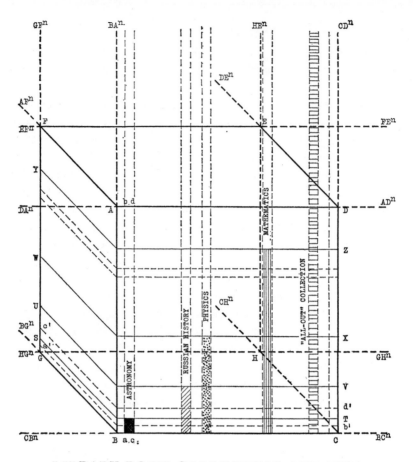

LIBRARY BOOK COLLECTING AND THE
WORLD OF THE WRITTEN RECORD

ST, UV, WX, and YZ, dividing the box—the world of "printed"
knowledge—into five unequal parts representing the degree or
levels of completeness to which a library collects.

The lowest section of the box, divided off by ST, represents a
purely minimal collection which contains only basic information,
general reading and reference material, and books to satisfy the
needs of introductory teaching. The blacked-in area of Figure 1
would stand for one such collection, astronomy, in one library.
The second higher level, marked off by UV, stands for a good
working collection capable of supporting *at least* the preliminary
investigations of graduate students and faculty. The diagonal
hatching represents one such subject, Russian history, in one
library. The dotted area, WX, indicates a subject, physics, in
which the library maintains a strong collection capable of supporting intensive research in many directions. Mathematics, the vertical
hatching, YZ, is a field for which the library provides a genuinely
comprehensive collection of research materials. The collection will
support most research, and is one of the best in the country.
Finally, for a very small number of fields or, more commonly,
subjects or topics—Franklin, Goethe, Risorgimento, Civil War, plant
pathology, Chinese painting, railroads, Herder, etc.—represented
by the horizontal hatching, the library strives for true completeness,
attempts to acquire everything it can of research value—both the
"bad" and the "good"—and aims at a collection second to none
anywhere.[15]

University libraries under the definition here used, will need to
maintain collections *at least* at the UV level in all the fields in
which the doctorate is offered, will strive for collections at the
WX level in most such fields, and aim at collections at the YZ
level in several.

(The box is, of course, an imperfect representation because, as
we have noted, fields of knowledge overlap in an almost infinite
number of ways and the lines between them are enormously
blurred; because degrees of completeness will never be precisely
definable in mathematical terms, and are therefore also blurred;
because in some subjects, as for instance mathematics or astronomy,
geographical subdivisions are meaningless and chronological ones

almost so; and finally, because it cannot simultaneously represent both a geographical and a chronological subdivision. Nonetheless, the figure may serve as a frame for certain images and ideas.)

It may be parenthetically granted here "that a good reference and working library for a university can be provided with a collection of 500,000 volumes." [16] But such a collection, as the author of the statement goes on to point out, cannot constitute the great, comprehensive scholarly library demanded by the research needs of faculty and graduate students in numerous disciplines. It is not a collection which brings prestige to a university. It is not the kind of collection which attracted great scholars to Columbia, Göttingen, Harvard, and Yale, and caused them to remain at these universities and others with outstanding research libraries. Presidents of universities with great libraries—Conant at Harvard, Ford at Minnesota, Hutchins at Chicago, Sproul and Kerr at California, and others—have publicly attested the drawing power of the library in attracting first-class scholars to their institutions. Less well known, perhaps, is this negative testimony of the president of the University of Illinois, contained in a statement to his Board of Trustees in 1912: "Speaking from an experience of eight years . . . I think I may say that I have had more people whom I have approached to consider positions at the University . . . decline . . . because of the lack of library facilities than for any other reason." [17] The statement would be an unlikely one today.

The university library of 500,000 volumes is not, above all, the kind of collection out of which great research flows and which makes possible the constant, steady pushing back of the frontiers of knowledge. For, though the library may contain all the useful bibliographies and finding lists, there is no way we can get around or ignore the indisputable fact, "That the standard measure of the value of a collection to the scholar engaged in research is its completeness," [18] and that "borrowing by interlibrary loan is a poor substitute for a good book collection; the potential value of a library to its users is determined almost entirely by its holdings." [19] It is not merely "a poor substitute," which might be tolerable. In the humanities and social sciences, at least, where the scholar may need to consult, some however briefly, literally thousands of items, immediacy of access to the great majority of needed material is indispensable. Without it, the delays, costs, and time limits of acquiring works from elsewhere make most productive scholarship impossible. It is not simply that the scholar wants this or that text, monograph, or article—mostly, given sufficient time, capable of being located and, if necessary, borrowed or photographed— he all too frequently wants a name, date, place, quotation, or figure. To locate just one such it may be necessary to run rapidly through fifty or a hundred references, not all of them known to him by author or title when he began his search. For such searches, taking place thousands of times daily in university libraries, there is no substitute for immediate access to a great collection. It is no longer physically possible, as it was in Johnson's day, that "a man will turn over half a library to make one book," [20] but he may very well "turn over" a large percentage of the holdings in certain sub-divisions of the classification system. Even from the viewpoint of the scientist, "A satisfactorily functioning research library must contain the material most likely to be needed by the researchers." [21] "It is then," as one scholar notes, "a proper and a central function of a university to enable its own faculty . . . to live and work as scholars. And this function is performed and must be performed primarily through the university library." [22] The faculty *cannot* "work as scholars" in small and limited collections. *If an institution is unable to provide a library capable of supporting most of the research of most of its faculty most of the time, it has no justification in claiming to be a university.* In the 1940s Rider, discussing then-current proposals for limiting the growth of research libraries, forcefully pointed out that all of them in some way or to some degree entailed the one concept intolerable to the scholar—taking his books away from him.[23] He is seldom satisfied by being told that the book he needs is more or less readily available "somewhere else" . . . "this demand for 'book immediateness,'" Rider notes, "is . . . nearly unanimous . . ." and ". . . [there is an] almost universal attitude of research workers toward the immediate ac-cessibility of their materials . . ." [24] The inevitable result of the acceptance of this position is ever more comprehensive—and larger—collections, whether they be in book, journal, near-print, microfilm, or microcard form, whether in conventional or compact storage.[25]

There is another point that deserves mention. Universities do not often contract, because the society they serve does not contract. They develop horizontally by embracing new fields, and vertically by intensifying their concern with fields already covered. We may then ask in what ways or at what points a library can safely be "selective." By neglecting those areas where the institution's research today is not in full flower? But the history of every university shows how rapidly these areas change, and when the change comes, the library is faced with the extraordinarily difficult and expensive task of building great strength quickly. By neglecting areas not now already strong? Again, an area weak today may need to be strong a few years hence. By being no more than "a good general working collection" at every point? Certainly not, for reasons already noted. Is the situation utterly hopeless then? No, not entirely. Legitimate and reasonably safe selectivity may be based upon, but only upon, the very highest administrative-faculty policy which says, in effect, but in detail: this institution does not now propose to undertake programs in fields A, B, C, D, . . . ; in fields . . . W, X, Y, Z it intends to attempt only minimal general and introductory work; in fields Alpha, Beta, Gamma, Delta . . . it will concentrate and specialize as follows. In all fields except those of A, B . . . and . . . WX . . . the library is bound to *aim toward* a degree of comprehensiveness. For most of these fields some selectivity is, of course, inescapable, if for no other than budgetary reasons but, to repeat, it is a selectivity which does not deny an *aim* toward comprehensiveness. The level at which each field will be maintained cannot be determined by the library alone but must be, as we have suggested, the result of joint library-faculty and, in so far as possible, of joint library-faculty-university administration decisions. Once such decisions have been reached, however, it should be the library's responsibility to make certain that agreed-upon levels, implied balances, and relative strengths as between subjects are maintained.

A generalization, not entirely fair though it is to a very few individual institutions, may be made here. It is that, in the area of faculty and administrative support for policy-making, the German libraries have been weak, and in areas of responsibility and authority for maintaining balance, the American libraries have been so.

The objections, on the part of many university administrators, as well as of some librarians, to the concept of the "aim toward comprehensiveness in many fields," and the resulting enormous, ever-growing university library, are recognized. These arguments are ones almost exclusively of expediency. Put baldly, they are arguments of cost for books, staff, and buildings. They have neither intellectual nor educational nor philosophical validity. It is to be observed, especially, that arguments for smaller or limited collections do not come from scholars who produce new knowledge, for whom the large collection is indispensable and for whom primarily the research materials have been built up and are maintained. The modern university thinks nothing, or very little, anyway, of paying up to fifty thousand dollars a month rental fee for a large computer, or of spending a few hundred thousand dollars for laboratory equipment, or half a million to a million or more dollars for a nucleus (atom) smasher which will be obsolete in five or ten years. Nor does the scientist apologize when he asks for larger, better, and costlier pieces of apparatus. The research library never becomes obsolete. The money devoted to building and maintaining it, produces a treasure which increases rather than diminishes with time. It is one of the university's very few assets the educational and monetary value of which compounds with the years and is greater than the sum of its parts; new additions gain value from their brothers and add to their value. Goethe's comment on the Göttingen Library is true for every university library and has even greater validity in the twentieth century than when he made it in 1801. "One feels as though in the presence of a great capital which silently spends its incalculable interest." [26] The library is the university's chief permanent investment. The library probably costs less to build and maintain than the aggregate of the laboratories, but it is the former, not the latter, which is indispensable to the entire university community. It is the laboratories, not the library, which obsolesce. Librarians are not responsible for any of the factors which cause great, costly, indefinitely expanding libraries, and they should in no wise be defensive about the fact that the institutions in their charge are very expensive and will unquestionably require, in the future, more rather than equal or less money, if the university expects distinction and if its scholars are to be properly served.

Proposals, which would put a relatively fixed upper limit, say one million or two million volumes, on the size of a university library's collection are, therefore, completely unrealistic.[27] One university's formal statement on this important point is worth quoting:

> The collection of the Berkeley Library is not and never will be a finished work. There has been found, over a long period, that a rate of growth of about 4% per year has made possible a sound and strong development. We think it would be risky to endanger this development by reducing that rate of growth. We see no reason to anticipate that our Library will require any less appropriation in the years to come, with all the changes in trends of research, new fields for study, and new opportunities for purchase of valuable materials that certainly will come.[28]

In the same document, the University librarian estimates that the Library will need to add a minimum of 1,250,000 volumes in the succeeding decade.[29] Or, as another institution puts it: "Everything that can be said about Harvard's book-collecting activities may be reduced to one simple proposition: qualitatively and quantitatively a high level of acquisition should be maintained." [30]

According to one compilation there were, world-wide, at the beginning of the 1950s, forty university libraries with collections of a million volumes or more.[31] Although the tabulation was not entirely accurate, the general picture is reliable enough. It is certain that the number of such libraries by the early 1960s was at least half again as many—Germany and America alone had, between them, more than thirty—and will continue steadily to increase. Does any faculty member of any of these institutions think his library too large? Does anyone believe significant amounts of the collection should be sold or given away? In the twenty-thirty collections of over 2,000,000 volumes would a professor in each of one hundred fields be willing to select, for permanent disposal, 10,000 volumes in *his* subject? Or 5,000?

We cannot place a limit on the size of the library, and it cannot fail to strive toward a degree of comprehensiveness in many fields. At the same time, almost paradoxically, it must pursue a policy of selectivity in all but a few fields where pre-eminent present strength and extraordinary research interest and activity, combined with available means, permit the library to say, In this subject we will buy every item we lack that becomes available, we have one of the three or four strongest collections in the world, and we intend to maintain that position.

How far in actual fact do the libraries go in an aim toward comprehensiveness? Further, it appears, than the printed literature would lead us to suppose.[32] Even the small and less wealthy libraries are likely to collect "all the way" in at least one subject; many do so in several; and the largest and wealthiest may claim half a dozen or more collections not surpassed and perhaps not equaled anywhere else. Thus, Louisiana State University takes it as its "duty . . . to obtain the finest and most complete library in the United States" in the field of sugar cane pathology.[33] Illinois attempts, for Carl Sandburg, Milton, and H. G. Wells, collections "including as far as possible all publications of research value . . . marginal materials . . . manuscripts, archives, ephemera." [34] Cornell buys "everything relating to the French Revolution" and covers "as intensively as possible the entire field of Proto-Renaissance and Renaissance cultural developments." [35] California's Bancroft, Chicago's folklore and Assyriology, Cologne's Thomas à Kempis, Columbia's typography, Cornell's Icelandiana, Duke's parapsychology, Frankfurt's Schopenhauer, Freiburg's Dante, Göttingen's Lichtenberg, Hamburg's Klopstock, Michigan's human ecology, Minnesota's Paul Bunyan and Scandinavian history and literature, Princeton's railroads, Texas's petroleum, UCLA's Dryden and Oscar Wilde, and Yale's Boswell-Johnson and Goethe, are among many other examples that might be mentioned.

But beyond these "all-out," or almost "all-out" collections, it is equally clear and of more general significance that all major universities, as well as many others, are continuously striving, within financial limitations, to build constantly more comprehensive collections in the fields of principal concern to their institutions.

In so far as choice must be made, and *some* choice is almost always necessary, Should a library prefer the new, current titles to the older? There are good arguments for answering the question either way.

For buying the new:

1. The demand for most books, even those of long-enduring scholarly value, has been shown to be greatest immediately after publication. If current books are not generously bought, the most immediate present interests and needs of the library's clientele will be unfulfilled; the library's position and the work of its users will seriously suffer. (Counter argument: Both the long-range value of, and the present need for, an older title may be greater than for the current one.)

2. The library can get more books for its money since it won't have to pay out-of-print prices, costs of telegrams, cables, etc.

3. Many books, not purchased on, or soon after, publication, will later be imperatively needed and will then be out-of-print, expensive and difficult, or impossible, to obtain.[36] (Counter argument: Copyflo, Xerox, etc., can make much research material readily available.)

4. If the library year by year does successfully the task of buying all important current publications, its out-of-print problems and costs will eventually become relatively fewer.

For emphasizing the older:

1. Despite the conscientious exercise of one's best judgment, many current books prove to have little permanent importance; therefore, monographs should not be purchased until time has proved their value. (Counter argument: If books are needed and useful today, they should be bought now, regardless of the judgment which time may render upon them.)

2. Some out-of-print titles, offered the library today, have been long sought, often for years. The opportunity to buy these and other out-of-print desiderata, if not seized today, may not come again; or, if it comes, the price is likely to be still higher.

3. Many, perhaps most, really important current books are likely to be available later on in reprinted or new editions, or in microreproduction. (Counter arguments: Every librarian can cite a list of needed works not so available; the later edition is sometimes not as good as the earlier; the various costs and difficulties involved in acquiring, maintaining, and using large collections of microreproduced material must be taken into account.)

Although, as partially suggested, some of these categorical statements are open to argument, it seems apparent that no final answer to the question is ever likely to be possible and that universally applicable generalization, ignoring a host of determining variables, is impracticable. The experience of the German libraries as a result of the two world wars is, however, pertinent. In 1914–1918 and 1940–1946 Germany was completely cut off from most foreign book markets. Despite the most strenuous efforts, and major financial support from the *Notgemeinschaft der Deutschen Wissenschaft* and its successor, the *Deutsche Forschungsgemeinschaft*, serious library lacks resulting from the two wars' isolation existed as late as the 1940s and the 1960s respectively. Programs for the purchase of foreign journal and monographic literature were begun in 1949 and 1951 respectively.

Thus, a man who happened to be working at the University of Göttingen on the question of book selection for university libraries, found that the library lacked, among other publications of the time, Numbers 1 and 2 of Volume VI (1945) of *College and Research Libraries*. The issues were out of print and unavailable by the time the end of World War II made possible the resumption of purchasing from abroad. In fact, some titles which the libraries would have purchased on publication immediately following World War I, when the catastrophic inflation had practically the same effect on the libraries' foreign acquisitions as the war itself, had still not been acquired forty years later.

This experience would seem to constitute a strong argument for a general emphasis on current publications—even if we optimistically assume that a future war will not again halt the international flow of print.

A further point arising out of the political and social developments of our time, may be observed. In the 1950s and early 1960s more than thirty new, independent countries came into being. It is almost inevitable that most of these countries will establish universities. Many have already done so. Among the dozens of universities created in such countries since World War II, may be mentioned the University of Ghana; the University of Karachi and Rajshahi University, Pakistan; the University of Libya; Bihar University and the University of Peshawar, India; the University of Dakar; the University of Ife, Nigeria; Bar Ilan University, Tel Aviv; the University of Sumatra; the University of Huê, Vietnam; and the University of the Ryukyus.

In addition, population and other pressures are forcing older nations to create new universities or to bring about the upward academic development of existing institutions. Michigan State College and Colorado Agricultural and Mechanical College have become state universities. The University of Łódź, the University Austral of Chile, the University of Chihuahua, Mexico, the Haile Selassie I University, and the University of the Saarland—to cite a few examples only—are post-World War II creations. West Germany is establishing three new universities, at Bochum, Bremen, and Regensburg, to provide for the enormously increased and rapidly growing student population.[37] For the same reason, California is swiftly developing three college campuses into full-fledged general universities and has created three new ones. England's so-called "red brick" institutions of higher education, a phenomenon of mid-twentieth century, have steadily increased in number and have become, or are developing into, true universities.

The point of all this is to suggest that the demand and competition for books is bound to increase in the years ahead.[38] The increase will be especially strong because many of the new and coming universities are in countries which, as yet, produce little in the way of general academic and scholarly literature. To be sure, the demand will be for almost all kinds of print, not simply current titles, of interest to universities. But the crux of the matter is that this expanded demand is certain to cause more current publications to go out of print faster, even though edition sizes will increase with demand.

Should a university library place its greater collecting emphasis upon the acquisition of books to fill "current" needs, expressed or supposed, or should its selection policy rather be more directed toward "building for the future"? From a strict point of view, "future" obviously means anything later than "now," and therefore applies to tomorrow, next week, next month, and next semester, as well as next year and five or ten years from now. Practically, "present" or "current" may equate with "expressed" or "assumed." Thus, the books a professor indicates he will need for a seminar he is to give, or a paper he expects to write next semester, may be held to constitute examples of both expressed and current need. When, however, the library buys a book without such an expression of either current or expressed (assumed) need, it must be buying for the future. In these terms the question is far from an academic one.

It may be granted at the outset that we are not likely ever to find a hard and fast answer to it. The instructional and research programs in different disciplines, the nature and status of collections supporting them, institutional policy for the present and future, available funds, the availability of desired literature (*e.g.*, there is little published today in Amharic, but may be much a decade or two hence); and a host of other variables prohibit categorical judgment.

It is, for example, clear that the more limited a library's funds, the less choice it will be called upon or privileged to make. Carried to the extreme, if the library's budget is sufficient *only* to supply demands resulting from immediate teaching and research needs, it will obviously have nothing to spend for the needs of the future. Conversely, a library with a very large book budget may have the best of two worlds by being able, at the same time, to acquire "everything" for which a specific need exists today and much which anticipates future need. Most university libraries fall between the two extremes.

The German library's more generally narrow, research-material-oriented collecting policy, discussed earlier in this chapter, results in the belief that most of what is acquired is being bought both for the present and the future. Some German librarians go so far as to maintain that this is virtually one hundred percent the case, and there is no reason to question their conviction. No American university librarian could take the same position since much of the secondary material for undergraduate teaching, recreational reading, and reserve book collections, however much used today, will be obsolete and of little or no value some years hence. Nonetheless, it seems clear, as Fussler has pointed out, "that book buying for a large research library tends to be very strongly oriented toward future or potential use, even in subject fields where the institution has a current and well established interest." [39] On the other hand, we may assume that a considerable proportion of the materials acquired by *any* university library, even that able only to fulfill today's needs, will be useful also in the future. The better the library, that is, the better its collection has been built up and the higher the quality of the material which has been acquired from day to day, the greater the proportion is likely to be. This does not, of course, mean, as has been pointed out in another connection, that the scholar fifty years from now will necessarily use a work for the same purpose as the scholar today. It does mean that the important piece of writing has enduring value.

It is axiomatic, also, that a work which gives some assurance of being able to satisfy future as well as current need is preferable to one which does only the latter. This leads to the conclusion that when choice is present, either as a possibility or necessity, the original account is better than the retelling of the account, the native text better than the translation, the first edition (generally) better than the reprint, the letters (generally) preferable to the biography based upon them, etc.

When we speak of "satisfying current demand" we should be quite clear that what is meant is not primarily the purchase of a book when someone needs it. On the contrary. What we mean, or should mean, is the library's supplying of the materials needed at this particular point in time. The scholar using the ideal book collection, built up by ideal day-to-day selection, (and with an ideal budget!) would theoretically never lack a single title; everything he required would already have been secured by the library in anticipation of his needs. This is a generally accepted view, both abroad and in the United States. "In principle, a properly set up library should anticipate the researcher's every wish, so that the books he needs are already available when he requests them." [40] The measure of the great libraries is that they approach this ideal.

As Redenbacher quite properly points out, "Inexcusable lacks would result if one were to follow the principle of waiting [to acquire material] until it was actually required or proposed for acquisition by the users." [41] No university library known to the writer buys exclusively on the basis of present expressed demand, though a few come unhappily close to doing so. On the other hand, American university library philosophy would question in part Redenbacher's juxtaposed dictum: "Immediate demand does not constitute for the scholarly library a determining criterion of acquisition; the need (*Bedarf*) of the day cannot, therefore, be made the foundation of selection." [42] If this view is carried to its logical conclusion (and unless the word *Bedarf* is given its secondary meaning of "desire" or "want," rather than "need"), the result is that the library puts itself in the position of claiming to know better than the user what he requires to do his work. Either that, or the library says, in effect, we will not (always) try to give you what you say you need. Either position seems from a broad philosophical and educational view, and entirely aside from any national considerations, quite untenable. Redenbacher later grants that, as "the object of use is a characteristic mark of the library, the value of utilization may be ignored only in exceptional cases." [43] But this concession would seem to most American librarians not to go far enough.

On the basis of logic as much as factual evidence then, we might say that the library should fulfill, by anticipation in so far as it can, the current teaching and research needs of its clientele; that it should do so, in so far as possible through the acquisition of materials having permanent value and maximum probable future usefulness; and that it should, additionally, to the extent of its financial ability, buy long-range on the basis of its knowledge of the library's strengths and weaknesses, of the institution's future program, of faculty interests, of research trends, and of the world literary output.

Nothing has thus far been said, and very little need be said, about the effects on a library's selection and collecting policy of cooperative measures and the proximity of other research collections. The discussion to this point has tacitly assumed that a university library will be largely sufficient unto itself, except that its need for some of the genuinely seldom-used, scarce, and unusual will be satisfied by interlibrary borrowing. This is often the fact; Cornell, Erlangen, Göttingen, Illinois, and Würzburg being, because of their relative geographic isolation and distance from other research libraries, fair examples. Very often, however, it is certainly not the fact. Munich, but a few blocks from the great Bavarian State Library, need not acquire research materials at the most intensive level in many fields *if* its students and faculty are accorded easy access to the State Library's collections.[44] The same is true of Marburg, almost next door to the *Westdeutsche Bibliothek,* containing nearly 2,000,000 volumes of the former Prussian State Library in Berlin. The cooperative arrangements between Duke and North Carolina; the University of Chicago and Northwestern (with, also, the Newberry and the John Crerar), and those embraced in the Midwest Inter-Library Center are too well known to need detailing here. Three points may be made. First, a library certainly need not buy the most specialized research materials if its clientele has ready access to them at another library in the locality; every library should, where possible, seek cooperative agreements of this kind which will increase its purchasing power, reduce the competition for scarce material, and further scholarship. Second, no library should expect another to bear the burden of its needs except for the rare, the unusual, and the relatively little used. A few university libraries on both sides of the Atlantic, readily admit that they do not have, on the average, 40–80 percent of the titles required for a dissertation. The justification for these universities offering work for the doctor's degree seems dubious. And third, the extent to which a library can afford not to acquire specialized research materials in fields of concern to its scholars, varies indirectly as the distance to a library which has those materials. No reasonable man will object to having to spend two hours in travel, or waiting a day or two (Princeton to Philadelphia or New York, Mainz to Frankfurt, Ann Arbor to Detroit, Stanford to Berkeley, Bonn to Cologne) once or twice a year. He will object mightily if he is asked to do so once or twice a week, and rightly so. And the greater and oftener his expenditure of time or the delay, the greater his objection. And rightly so. If his university cannot, most of the time, provide the materials which will enable him effectively to do his work as a scholar, it has no business pretending to be a research institution in the field.

TYPES AND SOURCES OF MATERIAL

A great deal of the writing on university library book selection is concerned with the types or forms of material—journals, microreproductions, rare books, newspapers, so-called ephemera, etc.—which a library should acquire; foreign versus native literature; bibliographical sources and criteria for the selection of individual titles; means of acquisition—purchase, of various kinds, including en bloc, gift, and exchange—and similar questions.[45] They are all of great importance to the acquisition program of the library. In the present view, however, as suggested at the beginning of the Introduction, they have nothing whatever to do with fundamental book-selection policy. That policy, in a single sentence, concerns the library's provision of the materials which will be of most value, now and in the future, for the needs of the library's users. The questions and matters just enumerated, therefore, are either of a peripheral, practical, or expedient nature; or, being concerned with the "getting" of material, are both practical and chronologically subsequent to the operation of selection. The issue here is: Does this graphic record contain material *which this library should have?* If this question is answered affirmatively, it matters not one particle whether the record is a book, a journal, a holograph letter, a newspaper, a map, or a

microfilm. It matters not one particle, except in the completely expedient matter of cost, whether it is purchased—or how, where, or
from whom—or acquired through gift or exchange. It matters not
one particle whether it is a single-sheet broadside or a ten-volume
set. And it matters not a particle whether the record is in English,
German, Japanese, or Polish—although, granted availability of the
material in the native language, this will, for obvious reasons, be
preferred.

In view, however, of the tremendous value to university libraries
of the materials which they receive through gift and exchange, additional brief comment on the topic may be desirable. Gifts have been
an important source of acquisitions from the very beginnings of
most libraries; exchanges no less so since at least the founding of
the learned and scientific societies in the seventeenth century. Increasingly, universities themselves have become major publishers,
much of the output being of prime scholarly value. The university
library is commonly given a number of copies, particularly of dissertations (when printed) and of official and scholarly serial publications, to exchange for similar items emanating from other institutions. A library may carry on as many as four thousand regular
exchanges, a quarter or more of them with institutions of higher
education. The vigorous prosecution of an exchange program is obviously much to the library's advantage in view of the quality of
the material received and the savings to the book budget. Very few
items secured through exchange are rejected. Yet, to repeat, the
criteria for the selection of gift and exchange material should be
exactly the same as for purchased material.

CHAPTER VI

Toward an "Ideal" Book Selection Policy

Despite the serious lacks and insufficiencies of present book-selection and collection-building policy and practice, there is considerable evidence to suggest that university libraries on the whole are now building better for the future than was the case seventy-five to a hundred and fifty years ago. Such a pessimistic view as the following seems quite unwarranted. "Our modern university libraries may be larger in volume, but there is no assurance that their qualitative value will be any greater in the twenty-first century than that of the average nineteenth century collection is for us." [1] Among the reasons and evidence for a more optimistic position may be cited the very real concern of virtually all present-day university librarians with the library's grave responsibility, and the generally far greater attention being given to the problems, policy, and practice of book selection.

Somewhat more tangible is the evidence that more people in libraries in Germany and in and out of libraries in America are spending time on the business of selecting books; that the international bibliographical apparatus even by the fourth quarter of the nineteenth century was generally not nearly so well developed as it is today; and that no American university library before about that time, and only a single German one before the beginning of the nineteenth century, consciously collected for research purposes *and* had the means effectively to do so. Up to approximately these two times, respectively, most German and American university libraries grew pretty largely like Topsy. For many now distinguished libraries, as we have seen in Chapters II and IV, a significantly different state of affairs came even later. Now, although the directions of university research will unquestionably change in the future, and although new fields of inquiry will arise, it seems improbable that

our fundamental view of research, its methods, and the materials
necessary for its prosecution will alter much, if at all. In other words,
the original account of a creative experiment, the governmental report on international credit balances, the author's autobiography, or
the first edition of a book of poetry, are likely to be as useful, though
perhaps not always for the same purposes, to the researcher fifty
years from now as they are to the scholar today. Further, the library
spending $100,000, or several times that sum, for books each year
is able to buy a larger proportion of the publications it believes important than could the library of a hundred years ago having annually only a few thousand, or a few hundred dollars.[2] If these propo-
sitions be granted, it seems certain that their combined effect will
be to produce for the worker of the twenty-first century resources
very much more generally useful than the collections of 1850 are
today.

Be this as it may, the evidence adduced in the previous chapters
seems clearly to suggest that present policy is somewhat deficient
and could be bettered. It is the purpose of this chapter to attempt
to outline the components of what might be defensible as an "ideal"
policy of book selection for university libraries. Several *caveats* and
apologiae need mention in advance.

The ideal is seldom a wholly, under all circumstances, feasible
and practicable solution to a problem. The more nearly the solution
approaches a true, philosophical, or logical ideal, the more likely
is this to be the case. This consideration does not constitute a justification for silence. Those who first proposed splitting the nucleus to
wrest from it an unlimited, that is, ideal, source of energy were no
doubt "impractical."

In the realm of ideas and of human institutions, in contradistinc-
tion, for example, to the laboratory investigation, conditions are
usually not duplicatable, and 1 plus 2 plus 3 do not always and
everywhere add up to 6. Even though it may be demonstrable that
the democratic institutions and practices of America may be the
best than can be devised for that country, it does not necessarily
follow that the very same institutions and practices *can* be inaugurated elsewhere or, if they can be, that they will produce comparable results. In other words, although the proposals suggested

here are believed to be generally, logically, and philosophically sound, it is not assumed that all of them could be adopted at all times, under all circumstances, and in all places.

The arguments and considerations which lead to this presentation have, in the main, been reviewed in the previous chapters and, in so far as that is the case, they are not repeated here.

Teaching and Research Policy Statement. The university administration, following consultation with, and advice from, appropriate academic groups, should provide the library with an official statement of policy, in some detail, as to the institution's present and probable future program of teaching and research. The statement should indicate the institution's level of interest in specific areas of learning, and the extent to which they will be supported and prosecuted. (*E.g.,* Middle Eastern languages, introductory work only; nuclear physics, comprehensive and intensive program, doctoral program, fullest possible support for faculty research.) Such a statement would need to be reviewed and revised at least every decade, possibly every five years. Without such a statement, carefully thought out, and known to all, a really effective long-range book selection and book collection building policy and program cannot be realized.

Development of a Level-of-Collecting Program. On the basis of this statement and with the cooperation of the faculty, a detailed level-of-collecting program should be developed within some such framework as that described in Chapter V. That is, conscious judgments, on a five-point scale, should be made and noted, for subjects and divisions of subjects indicating the level of collecting. To be genuinely useful and effective, these judgments should probably be rendered to the detail involved, for example, in the thousand major classifications of the Dewey system. The development of such a policy statement will obviously involve a good deal of work. It will involve less than might at first appear, however, since many judgments should result more or less automatically from the institutional policy statement described under the first heading. Decisions agreed upon as to level-of-collecting for various subjects should help to insure the building up of the library's collections in a balanced, coordinated fashion, and in conformity with the actual teaching and research program of the institution. The policy statement proposed here should be under fairly constant review and should certainly be reviewed as a whole not less frequently than once every five years. At any given time, however, relatively few collecting-level decisions would need to be substantially revised.

Budget and Book Selection Responsibility. The whole *responsibility* for selection and collection building, and the *entire* book budget, including book money for branch, departmental, divisional, institute, and seminar libraries, should reside, legally and actually, with the university library.

Library Staff Corps of Book Selectors. The major portion of the titles acquired by the library, or any branch, divisional, departmental, or institute library, should be, and would as a result be selected by members of the library staff—and well in advance of the clientele's need for them.

If the library has on its staff enough members with the highest subject and bibliographical knowledge, and if these individuals are given the responsibility and sufficient time for book selection, the result will be a more *objectively, consistently, thoroughly* built-up book collection than can otherwise be the case. Gone, or at very least far less operative, will be the influence of special or narrow interests, and of personal bias, ignorance of major parts of the collection as a whole, the often disastrous results of personnel changes or absences. For, with respect to book selection in such a framework, the library staff may be considered as an "administrative" continuum in a way that no academic individuals can be. The absence or change of a library staff member is immediately known to the library administration and steps can at once be taken to fill the gap. Not so the absence of, or change in, the putative professor-book selector who is a Civil War historian, an anthropologist, or a Gestalt psychologist. A library staff of this kind, in short, has the knowledge; the time; the fixed administrative duty and obligation; the immediate and constant access to the necessary bibliographical apparatus; the consistency of operation and viewpoint; the knowledge of a large segment of the collection; and, more than any others, the awareness "of the total problem of the relationship between the scholar and all of the resources of scholarship," [3] which appear to be the principal requirements, aside from adequate book funds, for the building up of scholarly libraries.

A library adding a total of 60,000 volumes a year (considerably fewer than the average of the "Princeton statistics" group) might have a cataloging staff of forty-five, of whom about twenty would be professional employees.[4] Many university libraries will, of course, have larger cataloging staffs; many, obviously, will have smaller ones. Columbia in 1956 had fifty-two and a half, of whom half were professional employees.[5]

The key to the contents of the modern library is its catalogs. But the key is only as valuable, so to speak, as the things to which it gives access. It seems logically possible, therefore, to suggest that libraries spend as much thought, time, and money in insuring the highest possible quality of the library's contents as they do in preparing the contents for use. Actually, an equal amount of money might not be necessary. A corps of twenty professional staff members with half as many clerical assistants might be sufficient. If twenty seems like an excessively large number for the tasks of selection, two considerations may be advanced. The first refers to the present German experience and practice, as described in the first half of Chapter III. Even the largest German group, of fifteen, is too small. The proposed corps should carry out substantially the same tasks as the German groups, plus the activity described under the next heading, and in America, at least, would be concerned with a considerably larger body of literature, as has been seen.

A variant plan to that of having a special, separate corps of book selectors would offer several advantages. Under this scheme, many, perhaps most of the professional staff would be assigned specific book selection responsibilities in accordance with their academic subject specializations. A fairly definite proportion of the staff members' working time would be available for the several activities which go to make up book selection. The entire program would be under the supervision of a small group of two or three coordinators, headed by a chief of book selection. Advanced and specialized subject competence of prospective staff would need to be a special consideration, to an extent much greater than it now generally is outside the European continent, in the recruitment of personnel for the library; it might be argued here, as it is argued on the Continent, that library staff book selectors should be as well prepared, academically, as the faculty they serve. A program of this kind, if it should embrace most professional members of present Anglo-American university library staffs, runs quite counter to the philosophy of most Continental scholarly libraries, including those of Germany, Holland, Austria, and the Scandinavian countries. These have long held that the task of book selection can be satisfactorily performed only by those who hold subject doctorates. The *Diplombibliothekar,* for example, in the German university library, though a library school graduate, is not deemed qualified for book selection and is given no responsibility for it. That this view is open to question is demonstrated by the outstanding collections which have been built up by such institutions as the New York Public Library and the British Museum where book selection is performed exclusively by large numbers of staff members few of whom hold the doctorate. It must be granted, however, that these individuals commonly have two to three more years of academic education than the *Diplombibliothekar* and his counterpart in libraries of other European countries.

The advantages of this variant are several. In the first place, it would benefit staff morale by giving many members of the professional group a share in responsibility for building the collection, that is, for the most important single activity in which the library engages. Second, in the same way, the attraction of sharing in this activity should be a strong positive factor in recruiting. Third, staff members not deemed by the library to have sufficiently advanced subject knowledge to participate in book selection would be provided with an additional incentive for further education and study in order to qualify for appointment to the group of selectors. Such appointment should be considered a matter of honor and prestige and should be clearly treated as such by the library. Fourth, in most university libraries, size of professional staff is such that subject assignments could be more narrowly made under this plan. With a staff of forty to one hundred or more, none might need to cover more than a single subject and some subjects, as for example history, might even be divided, one member being assigned Western European, one the United States, and so on. Staff interest, and attention to, and coverage of each field should, as a result, be greater than where one person had responsibility for an entire field or even two or three fields. Finally, there would be a financial advantage, in that such a program should cost less in staff salaries than would the setting up of a full-blown, separate corps of selection specialists per se.

Some, though not the major, aspects of this proposed program have been tried in a few American university libraries. Washington, (Seattle), for example, did so in the 1940s and 1950s. The staff, however, was organized through a committee system, bought no books less than five years old, and never had more than $3,000 at its disposal; and the subject knowledge of prospective staff members played no part in the recruitment of staff as potential book selectors.[6]

Faculty Participation in Book Selection. Faculty participation in selection should be encouraged and fostered and, especially, should be made more nearly universal than it is now. To this end the library staff book-selectors should be expected to devote possibly a fifth to a tenth of their total time, depending upon whether the special Library Staff Corps plan or its variant is adopted, to working with individual members of the faculty. In particular, new appointees, and those who have previously shown little or no concern for the library, should be visited, their interests discovered, their special bibliographic knowledge exploited, and offers of assistance and the strongest possible encouragement to active participation in book selection given. A program of this kind, pursued over a period of years, would result in personal acquaintance of the library staff members with most members of the faculty. Contact by mail and telephone, between personal visits, should be maintained. The closest possible contact with existing branch, departmental, divisional (or institute) libraries should also be maintained, and a maximum of collection-building coordination striven for. A special duty of the library staff members would be, in the light of the Teaching and Research Policy Statement, long-range study of predictable demands on the library, the present resources, and the resources required.

In order that this corps not work in a vacuum, isolated from other library activities, and in order that it have contact with general library problems, its members should likewise have line responsibilities which might take about one quarter of their time. If the variant plan were adopted, staff members with book selection responsibility might be spending upward of three quarters of their total working time on other duties.

Collections Built to Strength. In so far as the present and prospective institutional program permits, the university library should build on existing strengths. The argument:

A. It cannot hope to be maximally strong in all fields and subfields.

B. Therefore it must choose between (1) an aim toward genuine strength in a more or less limited number of fields and subfields, or (2) the division of available funds more or less equitably among all possible fields, with the result that none will have real distinction.

C. The library serves its institution in particular, and the world of scholarship in general, better if its collections permit extensive and intensive research in some, even though a very limited number of fields, than it does if it offers merely minimal to fair collections in many fields and excellent ones in none. No one will be attracted to, and no important work will be done in a library of the latter kind; some, at least, will be in a library of the former.

D. If the library pursues the program of (B 1) it will have limited success *unless* it builds on existing strength because (1) many basic, essential items will be difficult, expensive, or impossible to acquire; and (2) the task of building to excellence from limited or minimal holdings will require far more time, effort, and money than will the creation of excellence from relative strength. Nothing in the foregoing is intended to imply that a library should not build up to adequacy, or even to great strength an area deplorably weak vis à vis the university's instructional and research program.

E. It is not necessary that *every* university library provide materials for doctoral study and intensive faculty research in Sumerian art, Icelandic literature, the political history of Albania, the cultural anthropology of Nigeria, or Polynesian land shells. If it is not already moderately strong in such fields, the university would be well advised not to commence programs requiring the attempt to build major library collections in them. Deliberate forswearing, at the points where academic policy is created, has been an all too rare phenomenon of universities everywhere. "All the evident and subtle aspects of institutional identity, sovereignty, pride and competitiveness" [7] have, in fact, contributed to an opposite development. Downs makes the point thus: "As long as universities insist upon carrying on instruction and research in virtually every subject under the sun, frequently in competition with one another, the libraries will be expected to support these programs by providing materials and services. Limitations of fields, however, is a direction in which universities have been reluctant to move. The trend is almost invariably toward expansion, not retraction." [8]

Aim toward Comprehensiveness. On the other hand, in fields where strength already exists and where the institutional program is comprehensive and intensive, the library should aim toward the highest degree of excellence, qualitative and quantitative, that it can possibly afford, *with due regard to the ready availability of the resources of nearby libraries and the possibilities for cooperative effort.* In all such fields, the *aim* should be toward comprehensiveness. This should be interpreted as meaning that a very good case indeed would have to be made for *not* acquiring *any* item of the graphic record deemed to be of value and which the library can afford. Any other policy but ill serves scholarship, not only of the distant but also of the immediate future. It is not believed that any man is wise enough, or gifted with sufficient foresight, to say that any document (excepting only the wholly derivative) will not be of genuine importance to some scholar some time.

This does not mean abdication from the duty, responsibility, and privilege of selection. In all, perhaps, but the minutest subdivision of a field, the library must select, if for no other reason than that it cannot acquire everything. And certainly "some things are better than others." [9]

Current Publications versus Older Titles. Other things being more or less equal as, of course, they frequently are not, the library should prefer the current rather than the older title. Obviously this does not mean that the library would forego the opportunity to acquire a long-sought, intensely wanted out-of-print item in favor of a current, in-print volume which will undoubtedly also be readily available in the near future! Obviously, also, a library which has been unable to buy essential and fundamental works at the time of their publication (*e.g.*, because of subsequent founding of the institution, subsequent development of a field of interest, lack of access to the sources of supply) or has lost such items (*e.g.*, as a result of war, fire, flood) will need to pay *special* attention to the second-hand market. But major emphasis on current works, until all the useful ones have been acquired, is, as a general principle, preferable to a program which, buying extensively in the second-hand market, leaves insufficient funds for the purchase of current titles. The former policy, consistently pursued over a period of years, will eventually reduce the time and money which the library has to spend identifying, locating, and buying out-of-print items.

Needs of the Present and Needs of the Future. Because of its obligation to fulfill the requirements of its present clientele, the library *must* acquire in considerable part "for the needs of the present"; it must also, however, acquire for the "needs of the future"; for, if it does not now do so, unavailability of material will later prevent it from fully doing so.

A university's library is its most important and indispensable resource. The material quality of that resource is determined by the excellence of the book collection. The quality of the book collection depends in turn upon selection policy and practice. Any measures undertaken to improve that policy and practice will result in collections better suited to the university's educational and scholarly needs. Even the partial adoption of the proposals discussed above would, it seems certain, lead to improved collections.

NOTES

Abbreviations: The following abbreviations have been used for the most frequently cited sources in the notes:

CRL   *College and Research Libraries*
CU-Li Photographic copy in the Library, School of Librarianship, University of California, Berkeley, California
Hand. *Handbuch der Bibliothekswissenschaft,* 2d ed., edited by Georg Leyh (Wiesbaden, Harrassowitz, 1955–1961), unless noted otherwise
HLB   *Harvard Library Bulletin*
LJ   *Library Journal*
LQ   *Library Quarterly*
Letter   Letter or other personal communication, cited by author, institution, and date, now in the archives of the University of California Library
NfWB *Nachrichten für Wissenschaftliche Bibliotheken*
ZfBB *Zeitschrift für Bibliothekswesen und Bibliographie*
ZfB   *Zentralblatt für Bibliothekswesen*

INTRODUCTION

1. Keyes D. Metcalf, *Report on the Harvard University Library: A Study of Present and Prospective Problems* (Cambridge, Harvard University Library, 1955), p. 15.

2. "das erste wissenschaftliche Geschäft der Bibliothek." Emil Jacobs, "Adolf von Harnack," *ZfB,* XLVII (August–September, 1930), 367.

3. Herman H. Fussler, "The Bibliographer Working in a Broad Area of Knowledge," *CRL,* X (July, 1949), 199.

4. Keyes D. Metcalf, "Problems of Acquisition Policy in a University Library," *HLB,* IV (Autumn, 1950), 301.

5. Keyes D. Metcalf, "Harvard Faces its Library Problems," in *The Place of the Library in a University* (Cambridge, Harvard University Library, 1950), p. 38.

6. "Dafür zu sorgen, dass zur richtigen Zeit die richtigen Bücher gekauft werden, ist die wichtigste Aufgabe des Bibliothekars. Aus der riesigen Fülle auszuwählen—abzuwägen—mit Gefühl für Qualität und

Relationen zu entscheiden—das ist das schwere und schöne Amt des Bibliothekars." Walter Bauhuis, *Die Universitätsbibliothek Münster in den Jahren 1957/58 und 1958/59* (Münster, Westfalen, 1959), p. 14.

7. On the reduction of spatial growth through compact storage, see Herman H. Fussler and Julian L. Simon, *Patterns in the Use of Books in Large Research Libraries* (Chicago, University of Chicago Library, 1961), especially pp. 268–70 and Bibliography pp. 281–83.

8. Walter Bauhuis, "Zur Gegenwärtigen Lage der Universitätsbibliothek Münster" (Münster, 1957), p. 1. Mimeograph.

9. *Der Wiederaufbau der Staats- und Universitäts-Bibliothek Hamburg. 10. bis 12. Jahresbericht . . . 1954/55, 1955/56, 1956/57* (Hamburg, Staats- und Universitäts-Bibliothek, 1957), p. 27.

10. Metcalf, *Report on the Harvard University Library: A Study of Present and Prospective Problems,* p. 95.

11. Good historical and critical treatments of the universal library concept are lacking in English. Valuable discussions in German are those by Peter Karstedt, "Zur Soziologie der Bibliothekstypen," in *Libris et Litteris (Festschrift für Hermann Tiemann . . .)* (Hamburg, Maximilian-Gesellschaft, 1959), pp. 61–76; Fritz Redenbacher, "Die Erwerbung," *Hand.,* II, 119–28; Hermann Tiemann, "Das Problem der Universalbibliothek Heute," *NfWB,* VI (May, 1953), 166–77.

12. R. E. Barker, *Books For All* (Paris, UNESCO, 1956), pp. 18–21 and pictograph 2 following p. 56.

13. M. B. Iwinski, "La Statistique Internationale des Imprimés," *Bulletin de L'Institut International de Bibliographie,* XVI (1911), 1–139.

14. Merritt estimated a world book production of 15,377,276 titles by 1940. Le Roy C. Merritt, "The Administrative, Fiscal, and Quantitative Aspects of the Regional Union Catalog," in *Union Catalogs in the United States,* ed. by Robert B. Downs (Chicago, American Library Association, 1942), pp. 77–82.

15. See Bernard M. Fry, *Library Organization and Management of Technical Reports Literature* (Washington, D.C., Catholic University of America Press, 1953), pp. 8–9 for an estimate of 75,000 annual United States military-related technical reports.

16. Keyes D. Metcalf and Edwin E. Williams, "Acquisition Policies of the Harvard Library," *HLB,* VI (Winter, 1952), 23.

17. "Nur die Technik, Veterinärmedizin und Landwirtschaft (mit Ausnahme des Weinbaus) finden im allgemeinen keine Berücksichtigung." Hermann Fuchs, *Universitätsbibliothek Mainz: Wissensnötiges und Wissenswertes für den Benutzer* (Mainz, 1952), p. 2.

18. "Die Bibliothek erwirbt die wissenschaftlich wichtige Literatur aller Gebiete." Letter from Hermann Tiemann, librarian, Hamburg, May 13, 1961.

19. "Daher sind die Bibliotheken allein das sichere und bleibende Gedächtniss des menschlichen Geschlechts." *Sämtliche Werke,* Vol. VI: *Parerga und Paralipomena,* Vol. II (Leipzig, Brockhaus, 1939), par. 254, p. 515.

20. From conversation with the librarian.

21. Rollin A. Sawyer, "Book Selection in the Reference Department of the New York Public Library," *CRL,* VI (December, 1944), 20.

22. See Herbert B. Adams, "Seminary Libraries and University Extension," *Johns Hopkins University Studies in Historical and Political Science,* XI (1887), 5th series, 443–69, especially pp. 448–56.

23. Zella Allen Dixson, "The Departmental Libraries of the University of Chicago," *LJ,* XX (November, 1895), 375. See also, as one of several similar instances, Henry O. Severance, *History of the Library, University of Missouri* (Columbia, University of Missouri, 1928), p. 60. Severance reported that in 1900 the total holdings of 30,000 volumes were located in fifteen separate libraries.

24. See Mary Irwin, ed., *American Universities and Colleges,* 8th ed. (Washington, D.C., American Council on Education, 1960), pp. 1160–62. Another kind of estimate of the number of "major" universities is suggested by the fact that, in 1959–1960, of Federal expenditures for research in two hundred eighty-seven institutions, twenty received 79 percent and sixty-six received 92 percent of the total. See Carnegie Foundation for the Advancement of Teaching, Advisory Committee for Study of the Federal Government and Higher Education, "Magnitudes and Interpretations of Involvement of Federal Agencies with Higher Education," *Staff Paper* (1961), p. 4. Mimeograph.

25. "Die englische und amerikanische Literatur über *book selection* bezieht sich so gut wie ausschliesslich auf *public libraries* und kann hier ausser Betracht bleiben." Fritz Redenbacher, "Die Erwerbung," *Hand.,* II, 113.

26. *Hand.,* II, 113–78. Redenbacher's contribution is a greatly expanded and revised reworking of Emil Gratzl's "Die Erwerbung," *Hand.,* 1st ed., II, 116–96.

27. *Hand.,* II, 150, Note 1. "It is striking that only a very few libraries have laid down written acquisition programs and in still fewer cases have these been made public." ("Es ist auffallend, dass ein Erwerbungsprogramm nur von ganz wenigen Bibliotheken schriftlich niedergelegt und in noch selteneren Fällen der Öffentlichkeit bekanntgegeben wurde.") The citations Redenbacher gives of individual policies are all printed and, with one exception, are not of university libraries. None is German. See Harry Bach, "Acquisition Policy in the American Academic Library," *CRL,* XVIII (November, 1957), 441–51. Bach discusses the arguments pro and con the drafting of formal policies. See also William

T. Henderson, "Acquisition Policies of Academic and Research Libraries" (Unpublished Master's thesis, Graduate Library School, University of Chicago, 1960).

28. Letter from Frederick H. Wagman, director of libraries, Michigan, November 14, 1955.

29. The data, based upon a summary of the replies Lewis C. Branscomb received, are used with his kind permission.

30. See Herman H. Fussler, "The Larger University Library," *CRL,* XIV (October, 1953), 363.

31. *Cf.* William R. Pullen, "Selective Acquisitions at Yale," in *Studies in Library Administrative Problems,* ed. by Keyes D. Metcalf (New Brunswick, N.J., Rutgers University, Graduate School of Library Service, 1960), p. 33.

I: THE UNIVERSITY, THE LIBRARY, BOOK SELECTION, AND BOOK COLLECTIONS

1. Ernest H. Wilkins, "The University Library and Scholarship," *HLB,* IV (Winter, 1950), 16.

2. Guy Stanton Ford, *On and Off the Campus* (Minneapolis, University of Minnesota Press, c. 1938), p. 359.

3. Viscount R. B. Haldane, *Universities and National Life* (London, Murray, 1912), p. 29.

4. See B. Sticker, "Das Wissenschaftliche Buch im Rahmen der Gesamten Bucherzeugung," in *Börsenblatt für den Deutschen Buchhandel* (Frankfurter Ausgabe, Jg. 11, Nr. 54, July 8, 1955), pp. 433–38. A classification of "scholarly" and "nonscholarly" types of books is suggested. In the latter category are included, among others, travel guides, general biographies, phrase books, popular science literature, school texts, and manuals.

5. See University Library Council, *Acceleration and Impact: Annual Report of the Libraries of the University of California, 1957/58* (Berkeley, University of California, 1958), pp. 4–5.

6. Harvard University Library, *Annual Report for the Year 1959/60* (Cambridge, Harvard University Library, 1960), p. 39.

7. *Ibid.,* p. 36.

8. University of California Academic Senate (Northern Section), "General Collecting Policy for the General Library, 1945–1946," p. 4. Mimeograph and map. Letter from Donald Coney, librarian, California, January, 1961.

9. Cornell University Library, "Outline of an Acquisition Policy" (Ithaca, N.Y., 1953), p. 2. Mimeograph.

10. Herman H. Fussler, "The Larger University Library," *CRL*, XIV (October, 1953), 364–65.

11. Columbia University, "Report of the Subcommittee Authorized by the Joint Committee on Graduate Instruction" (New York, 1948), p. 2. Mimeograph.

12. University of Illinois Library, "Acquisition Policy Statement" (Urbana, February, 1959), p. 1. Mimeograph.

13. American Library Association and Association of College and Reference Libraries, College and University Post-War Planning Committee, *College and University Libraries and Librarianship* (Chicago, American Library Association, 1946), p. 48.

II: EARLY COLLECTING AND COLLECTIONS

1. Some writers give the contrary impression. Joris Vorstius, for example, speaks of the rapid increase of university library holdings in the middle half of the nineteenth century, citing Göttingen's and Leipzig's increases from 200,000 to 400,000 volumes and 50,000 to 350,000 volumes, respectively, from 1822 to 1875. He has, however, chosen two of the three largest to make his point. Reference to Tables 1 and 2 shows that, although about a third of the libraries did indeed increase very substantially, both in absolute and percentage terms between 1850 and 1875, only four held as much as 5 percent of total world book output by the latter date. Joris Vorstius, *Grundzüge der Bibliotheksgeschichte*, 5th ed. (Leipzig, Harrassowitz, 1954), p. 77.

2. See, for example, Charles Franklin Thwing, *The American and the German University* (New York, Macmillan, 1928).

3. *Cf.* Georg Leyh, "Die Deutschen Bibliotheken von der Aufklärung bis zur Gegenwart," *Hand.*, III, Pt. 2, pp. 86–96, 229–44.

4. Other major developments of the century were the secularization of the monasteries in 1802–1803, the libraries of many of which went to universities; extensive catalog reforms; new, use-oriented buildings; and the emergence of the professional librarian.

5. Extensive citation here seems unnecessary. The facts are documentable from original records and are readily available in numerous research studies and secondary sources. See Rudolf Bülck, *Geschichte der Kieler Universitätsbibliothek* (Eutin, Burkhardt, 1960); Otto Handwerker, *Geschichte der Würzburger Universitäts-Bibliothek bis zur Säkularisation* (Dissertation, Würzburg, Stürtz, 1904), p. 130; Georg Leyh, *Hand.*, III, Pt. 2, pp. 86–88; Otto Mitius, *Die Bibliothek der Universität Erlangen: ein Geschichtlicher Überblick* (Erlangen, Junge, 1925), pp. 10, 12; Bernard Weissenborn, "Die Hallische Universitätsbibliothek während der 250 Jahre," in *250 Jahre Universität Halle* (Halle, Niemeyer, 1944).

6. Louis Shores, *Origins of the American College Library, 1638–1800* (Nashville, George Peabody College, 1934), pp. 101, 109; see also, pp. 50–101 for details on the small size and indifferent quality of the collections.

7. Charles C. Jewett, *Notices of Public Libraries in the United States of America* (Washington, D.C., 1851), p. 31. As relatively late as 1825 Columbia's Library expenditures were $177.44. Nicholas Murray Butler, "The Libraries of Columbia," in *South Hall: Columbia University, New York* (New York, Columbia University, 1935), p. 3.

8. Gotthold Ephraim Lessing, *Zur Geschichte und Litteratur. Aus den Schätzen der Herzoglichen Bibliothek zu Wolfenbüttel* (Erster Beytrag, Braunschweig, Waysenhaus, 1773), p. 3 ff. This is a scarce publication, listed in Kayser but not in Heinsius. The work, and three succeeding *Beiträge*, are often omitted from so-called "complete" or "collected" editions of Lessing. All four contributions may be found in Karl Lachmann's edition, *Sämtliche Schriften* (Stuttgart, Göschen, [XI] 1895 and [XII] 1897). The reference appears, XI, 319.

9. The literature on the founding and development of the University is exceedingly voluminous and comprises more than two hundred fifty separate monographs and articles. It seems likely that the history of no other university is better documented. Only a few of the more comprehensive and readily accessible titles, with special reference to the Library, are cited here. Karl Julius Hartmann, ed., *Vier Dokumente zur Geschichte der Universitäts-Bibliothek Göttingen* (Hainbergschriften IV) (Göttingen, Häntzschel, 1937); Karl Julius Hartmann and Hans Füchsel, *Geschichte der Göttinger Universitäts-Bibliothek* (Göttingen, Vandenhoeck and Ruprecht, 1937), with an eleven-page Bibliography; Alfred Hessel, *Leibniz und die Anfänge der Göttinger Bibliothek* (*Vorarbeiten zur Geschichte der Göttinger Universität und Bibliothek*, III) (Göttingen, Pillai, 1924); Samuel Christian Hollmann, *Die Georg-Augustus-Universität zu Göttingen in der Wiege, in ihrer Blüte und Reiferem Alter; Fragment einer Geschichte der Georg-Augustus-Universität zu Göttingen* (Göttingen, 1787); Georg Leyh, "Die Göttinger Bibliothek in den Grundzügen ihrer Entwicklung," *Nordisk Tidskrift för Bok-och Biblioteksväsen*, XXXVI (1949), 69–89; Georg Leyh, "Zur Vorgeschichte der Modernen Wissenschaftlichen Bibliothek in Deutschland," *Libri*, IV (1954), 193–202; Johann Stephan Pütter, *et al.*, *Versuch einer Academischen Gelehrten-Geschichte von der Georg-Augustus-Universität zu Göttingen* (4 vols., Göttingen, Hannover, 1765–1838), Library: I, 210–24, II, 213–32, III, 398–419, IV, 80–90; Emil F. Rössler, *Die Gründung der Universität Göttingen: Entwürfe, Berichte und Briefe der Zeitgenossen* (Göttingen, Vandenhoeck and Ruprecht, 1855); Götz von Selle, *Die Georg-August-Universität zu Göttingen, 1737–1937* (Göttingen, Vandenhoeck and Ruprecht, 1937); F. W. Unger, *Göttingen und die Georgia*

Augusta (Göttingen, Deuerlich, 1861); University of Göttingen Library, *Beiträge zur Göttinger Bibliotheks- und Gelehrtengeschichte (Vorarbeiten zur Geschichte der Göttinger Universität und Bibliothek,* No. 5). (Göttingen, Vandenhoeck and Ruprecht, 1928).

10. *Cf.* Fritz Milkau, "Die Bibliotheken," in *Die Allgemeinen Grundlagen der Kultur der Gegenwart* in *Die Kultur der Gegenwart, ihre Entwickelung und ihre Ziele,* ed. by Paul Hinneberg (Berlin and Leipzig, Teubner, 1906), Pt. I, sec. 1, p. 556.

11. *Ibid.,* p. 553; Vorstius, *Grundzüge der Bibliotheksgeschichte,* p. 57.

12. Pütter, *Versuch einer academischen Gelehrten-Geschichte von der Georg-Augustus-Universität zu Göttingen,* IV, 81–82.

13. See Hartmann, *Vier Dokumente zur Geschichte der Universitäts-Bibliothek Göttingen,* p. 19; Pütter, *Versuch einer academischen Gelehrten-Geschichte von der Georg-Augustus-Universität zu Göttingen,* I, 210–11.

14. *Ibid.,* III, 401. In I, 214–18, he gives an impressive selected list of important holdings of the 1760s.

15. *Ibid.,* IV, 83.

16. See, for example, among many others, Friedrich Gedike's commendatory judgment in Richard Fester, *"Der Universitäts-Bereiser," Friedrich Gedike und Sein Bericht an Friedrich Wilhelm II.* (Berlin, Duncker, 1905), pp. 26–27.

17. Pütter, *Versuch einer academischen Gelehrten-Geschichte von der Georg-Augustus-Universität zu Göttingen,* I, 213, 219, III, 409–11.

18. "Gesetze der Bibliothec zu Göttingen," 28. Oktober 1761, in Archives of the Kurator, University of Göttingen. See Georg Leyh, "Die Gesetze der Universitätsbibliothek zu Göttingen vom 28. Oktober 1761," *ZfB,* XXXVII (January–February, 1920), 1–30.

19. Arnold Herrmann Ludwig Heeren, *Christian Gottlob Heyne* (Historische Werke, Part 6) (Göttingen, Rower, 1823), p. 229.

20. Pütter, *Versuch einer academischen Gelehrten-Geschichte von der Georg-Augustus-Universität zu Göttingen,* I, 212–13.

21. "von dem Direktor . . . hat man bisher gefordert, dass er den grossen Umfang des literarischen und wissenschaftlichen [Geschäfts?] dieses Instituts besorge und ihnen [sic!] einen grossen Theil seiner Kräfte und seiner Zeit widme. Um dieses zu können, muss er die ganze Literatur aller Zeiten übersehen; er muss wissen, was in jedem Theil wichtiges geschrieben und gedruckt, wie viel davon bereits in der Bibliothek vorhanden oder noch anzuschaffen ist. Er muss also nicht nur die neue und neueste deutsche, sondern die ganze europäische Literatur in ihrem Umfange kennen. . . . Dazu ist eine fortgesetzte Lectüre von Literarischen Blättern und Aufmerksamkeit auf wichtige Bücher-Auctionen erforderlich . . . der Bibliothekar muss die neuen Producte so kennen, dass er weiss, ob und welche Schriften in den wissenschaftlichen Plan

der ihm anvertrauten Bibliothek gehören, und die Wissenschaft weiter gebracht haben. . . . Die hiesige Universitäts-Bibliothek ist kein Bücherladen, keine Liebhaber- und keine Hofbibliothek. Sie enthält . . . Bücher aus allen Wissenschaften und Sprachen—aus allen die wichtigsten für die Wissenschaft, und für die in derselben Arbeitenden. Nur durch Befolgung dieser Verwaltungsgesetze . . . konnten die Vorzüge erwachsen, welche die Bewunderung der . . . Bibliothek erweckt, und sie zur ersten von Europa in ihrer Art gemacht haben.

"dass in Hinsicht auf die neueste Literatur aller europäischen Nationen die hiesige Bibliothek sich ohne Unbescheidenheit die ausgesuchteste in der Welt nennen darf." University of Göttingen Library, ms. Bibliotheks-Archiv 24. C, 13. Reproduced in *Ein Bericht Heynes aus der Westfälischen Zeit und Seine Programmatische Bedeutung (Vorarbeiten zur Geschichte der Göttinger Universität und Bibliothek. No. 1.)*, ed. by Richard Fick (Göttingen, Pillai, 1924), pp. 11–15.

22. "Alles dasjenige, was eigentlich hieher gehoert, ist ein liberaler Aufwand, welcher erfordert wird, theils zur Erhaltung dessen, was bereits vorhanden ist, theils zur regelmaessigen Fortsetzung durch einen immer fortgehenden Ankauf bey der taeglich fortschreitenden Litteratur so vieler cultivirten Nationen; damit in diesem unschaetzbaren Schatze der menschlichen Kenntnisse keine Luecken entstehen, welche mit der Zeit den unermesslichen Werth des Ganzen gar sehr vermindern wuerden.

"Die Zahl der Buecher ist das, was am wenigsten in Betrachtung koemmt; den wahren Werth macht die zweckmaessige Auswahl fuer eine Universitaet.

"die weitere Fortsetzung, damit keine Luecken entstehen, erfordert ununterbrochene planmaessige Anschaffung desjenigen, was, bey der immer fortschreitenden wissenschaftlichen Cultur, aus dem taeglich erscheinenden neuen Anwachse der einheimischen und auslaendischen Litteratur noethig ist fuer eine Bibliothek, welche fuer einen wissenschaftlichen Plan . . . nach Inbegriff und Umfassung der wichtigsten Schriften aller Zeiten und Voelker in allen Wissenschaften, in einheimischer und auslaendischer Litteratur, eingerichtet ist." *Goettingische Gelehrte Anzeigen,* I (May, 1810), 849–52. Reproduced, although not with complete accuracy, in *Vier Dokumente zur Geschichte der Universitäts-Bibliothek Göttingen,* ed. by Hartmann, pp. 14–18.

23. Letter from Jacob Grimm to the *Kuratorium* (Board of Trustees), January 15, 1833 (Göttingen, Kur. Arch. 4 V d 1. Nr. 44). Reproduced in *Vier Dokumente zur Geschichte der Universitäts-Bibliothek Göttingen,* ed. by Hartmann, pp. 28–29.

24. An account, inaccurate in some details, and now rather out of date, appears in Margaret Burton, *Famous Libraries of the World* (London, Grafton, 1937), pp. 189–206.

25. See Leyh, *Hand.,* III, Pt. 2, pp. 239–41. An illuminating chron-

ological tabulation of Marburg's book budgets, 1527–1889, is appended
to Gottfried Zedler, *Geschichte der Universitätsbibliothek zu Marburg
von 1527–1887* (Marburg, Elwert, 1896), pp. 162–63. Before 1850 the
regular budget never exceeded 3,200 taler ($2,880); before 1875, 4,200
taler ($3,780).

26. *Cf.* Klemens Löffler, "Das Erbe der Stifts- und Klosterbibliotheken
in den Öffentlichen Bibliotheken Deutschlands," *St. Wiborada*, I (1933),
55–92.

27. *Cf.* M. B. Iwinski, "La Statistique Internationale des Imprimés,"
Bulletin de L'Institut International de Bibliographie, XVI (1911), 6.

28. (Section 1) "Die Königl. Universitäts-Bibliothek als unentbehr-
liches literarisches Hülfsmittel für die Zwecke der Universität soll den
Geist wahrer Wissenschaft und Kunst befördern, und ein mit allseitiger
Umsicht angelegtes Archiv ihrer Werke seyn."

(Section 2) "Sie schliesst daher alles Werthlose, Geringfügige und
Entbehrliche aus, *was blose Neugierde oder Wünsche des Anfängers
und des Ungelehrten befriedigen kann;* es sey denn, dass sie solches
Geschenken verdankte."

(Section 4) "Werke, die einen vorzüglichen und bleibenden Werth
haben, sollen in keinem Fache vernachlässigt, und die in irgend einem
Fache fehlenden Hauptwerke bei vorkommender Gelegenheit nachgeschafft werden."

(Section 6) "Originale gehen den Übersetzungen vor, und letztere
verdienen nur dann eine Stelle auf einer Universitäts-Bibliothek, wenn
sie ein *bestimmtes Interesse für die Kunst oder die Wissenschaft haben.
Erleichterung des Verständnisses eines Schriftstellers für Anfänger ist
keine Rücksicht, welche bei einer Universitäts-Bibliothek in Betrachtung
kömmt.*"

(Section 10) "In der schönen Literatur sind classische Werke aller
Nationen überhaupt und der vaterländischen Literatur insbesondere
allein regelmässig zu berücksichtigen, und ausser diesen *nur solche,
welche entweder in ihrer Entstehung, oder in ihrer Wirkung eine bleibende Bedeutung durch den Zeitgeist erhalten haben.*" (italics added)
Bibliotheks-Ordnung der Königlich. Bayerischen Universität zu Erlangen.
(Erlangen, gedruckt mit Junge'schen Schriften, 1826), pp. 1, 4 (CU-
Li). Reproduced in *Serapeum*, VIII, *Intelligenz-Blatt*, Nos. 4, 5, and 6
(1847), 25–28, 33–37, and 41–45.

29. "so werden die Fakultäten selbst ermessen, dass sie insbesondere
ihre Vorschläge auf Hauptwerke . . . und solche, die einen wissenschaftlichen Zweck haben, einzuschränken, Bedacht nehmen, . . . un-
bedeutende dagegen, die jeder Professor sich selbst anschaffen kann [!],
und solche, welche etwa nur zur Unterhaltung dienen, ganz ausschliessen.
Der Hauptgesichtspunkt muss sein, dass . . . kein wichtiges wissenschaftliches Hauptwerk darin fehle." *Reglement der Königlichen Bi-*

bliothek zu Königsberg vom 17. October, 1822 (CU-Li). Reproduced in *Serapeum,* VII, *Intelligenz-Blatt,* No. 7 (April 15, 1846), 52.

30. "Es soll . . . auf Anschaffung solcher Schriften Bedacht genommen werden, welche Quellen und Hülfsmittel für wissenschaftliche Forschungen darbieten oder wichtige Resultate gründlicher Studien und Beobachtungen enthalten.

"Lehrbücher und ähnliche Schriften, welche Lehrer und Studirende in ihrer Privatbibliothek besitzen müssen, oder Werke, von denen wiederholt veränderte Auflagen zu erwarten sind, sollen nur dann angeschafft werden, wenn in ihnen die Ergebnisse sehr einflussreicher wissenschaftlicher Forschungen niedergelegt sind. Leere Prachtwerke, Schriften, welche bloss Unterhaltung gewähren oder von ephemerem politischen Interesse sind, sollen niemals angeschafft werden." *Regulativ über die Benutzung der Universitäts-Bibliothek zu Rostock vom 21. September 1840* (CU-Li). Reproduced in *Serapeum,* VII, *Intelligenz-Blatt,* No. 19 (October 15, 1846), 147–48.

31. "Anschaffung von Werken, welche ein allgemeines wissenschaftliches Interesse haben. . . . Es müssen . . . diejenigen Schriften, welche zu jeder Zeit in der Wissenschaft Epoche gemacht haben, überhaupt nur Werke von bleibendem Werthe . . . vorhanden sein." *Instruction für die Bibliothekscommission,* par. 7b and c, in *Chronologische Sammlung der im Jahre 1826 Ergangenen Verordnungen und Verfügungen für die Herzogthümer Schleswig und Holstein* (Kiel, 1827), p. 194 (CU-Li). The Library regulations are reproduced under the title, *Ordnung der Universitätsbibliothek zu Kiel,* 1826 (CU-Li). Reproduced in *Serapeum,* VIII, *Intelligenz-Blatt,* No. 1 (January 15, 1847), 3.

32. "Bei Anschaffung neuer Werke ist . . . auf die möglichste literarische Vollständigkeit jedes Fachs, ohne Zurücksetzung einzelner Fächer oder Vorliebe für andere, Rücksicht zu nehmen." *Reglement für die Königliche und Universitäts-Bibliothek zu Breslau vom 19. Mai 1815,* Article III, par. 1. Reproduced in *Serapeum,* VI, *Intelligenz-Blatt,* No. 14 (July 31, 1845), 107.

33. *Reglement für die Universitätsbibliothek zu Bonn vom 25. August 1819,* Article III, par. 1. Reproduced in *Serapeum,* VI, *Intelligenz-Blatt,* No. 9 (May 15, 1845), 65. (Original ms., Bonn, has the title *Reglement für die Bibliothek der Königlich Preussischen Universität zu Bonn.*)

34. "Werke, die einen vorzüglichen und bleibenden Werth haben, sollen in keinem Fache vernachlässigt, und die in irgend einem Fache fehlenden Hauptwerke bei vorkommender Gelegenheit nachgeschafft werden." *Bibliotheks-Ordnung der Königlich Bayerischen Universität zu Erlangen,* p. 1.

35. "mit den Anforderungen der einzelnen wissenschaftlichen Zweige und den Fonds zur Bestreitung der Auswahl in ein richtiges Verhältniss zu bringen . . . [und] dass möglichste literarische Vollständigkeit jedes

Fachs erreicht, Zurücksetzung einzelner Fächer oder Vorliebe für andere stets vermieden werde." *Verordnung für die Bibliothek der Grossher-zoglichen Ludewigs-Universität zu Giessen.* 8. November 1837, par. 15 (CU-Li). Reproduced in *Serapeum,* V, *Intelligenz-Blatt,* No. 21 (November 15, 1844), 164.

36. "Für die verschiedenen Fakultätswissenschaften und deren Haupt-zweige muss auf eine möglichst gleichförmige Weise gesorgt werden, wobei jedoch für diejenigen Fächer, die am meisten einer Vervollständi-gung bedürfen, zuvörderst und baldmöglichst Sorge zu tragen ist." *In-struction für die Bibliothekscommission,* par. 7a in *Chronologische Samm-lung der im Jahre 1826 Ergangenen Verordnungen und Verfügungen für die Herzogthümer Schleswig und Holstein,* pp. 193–94. Reproduced in *Ordnung der Universitätsbibliothek zu Kiel,* 1826 (CU-Li). Repro-duced in *Serapeum,* VIII, *Intelligenz-Blatt,* No. 1 (January 15, 1847), 2–3.

37. *Instruction für die Bibliothekscommission,* par. 7 and 8 in *Chrono-logische Sammlung der im Jahre 1826 Ergangenen Verordnungen und Verfügungen für die Herzogthümer Schleswig und Holstein,* pp. 193–96. Reproduced in *Ordnung der Universitätsbibliothek zu Kiel,* 1826 (CU-Li). Reproduced in *Serapeum,* VIII, *Intelligenz-Blatt,* Nos. 1, 2, 3 (1847), 1–6, 9–14, 17–22. See also Bülck, *Geschichte der Kieler Uni-versitätsbibliothek,* pp. 130–31, 208.

38. *Verordnung für die Bibliothek der Grossherzoglichen Ludewigs-Universität zu Giessen,* par. 11, 14, 16 (CU-Li). Reproduced in *Serapeum,* V, *Intelligenz-Blatt,* No. 21 (November 15, 1844), 163, 164.

39. *Cf.* Julius Steup, "Geschichte der Universitäts-Bibliothek Seit 1852," in *Die Universität Freiburg Seit dem Regierungsantritt . . . des Grossherzogs Friedrich von Baden* (Freiburg und Tübingen, Mohr, 1881), pp. 75–79.

40. *Bibliotheks-Ordnung der Königlich Bayerischen Universität zu Erlangen,* pp. 5–6.

41. *Reglement der Königlichen Bibliothek zu Königsberg vom 17. October 1822* (CU-Li). Reproduced in *Serapeum,* VII, *Intelligenz-Blatt,* No. 7 (April 15, 1846), 42, 50, 51.

42. "Das Bibliothekariat darf niemals ohne Wissen und ohne schrift-liche Genehmigung des Verwalters einer Rate aus derselben Verwendun-gen für die Universitäts-Bibliothek machen." *Regulativ über die Benut-zung der Universitäts-Bibliothek zu Rostock vom 21. September 1840* (CU-Li). Reproduced in *Serapeum,* VII, *Intelligenz-Blatt,* No. 19 (Octo-ber 15, 1846), 146, 149, 154.

43. *Verordnung für die Bibliothek der Grossherzoglichen Ludewigs-Universität zu Giessen,* par. 19. Reproduced in *Serapeum,* V, *Intelligenz-Blatt,* No. 22 (November 30, 1844), 170–71.

44. *Bibliotheksordnung der Königlich Bayerischen Universität zu*

Erlangen (Erlangen, Junge & Sohn, 1903), p. 1. Reprinted in *ZfB*, XXI (August-September, 1904), 406–9.

45. ["Die Ordnung] konserviert das alte Ratensystem, das die Bibliothek in einzelne Abteilungen zerreisst und jede gesunde Anschaffungspolitik unmöglich macht." *Ibid.*, p. 409.

46. *Bestimmungen über die Vermehrung der Universitäts-Bibliothek* (Rostock, Univ.-Buchdr. 1904). Reprinted in *ZfB*, XXI (December, 1904), 562–64.

47. *Bestimmungen über die Verwaltung und die Benutzung der Grossherzogl. Universitäts-Bibliothek zu Giessen.* (Giessen, v. Münchow'sche Hof- und Univ.-Druckerei, 1904). Reprinted, in part, in *ZfB*, XXI (December, 1904), 564–65.

48. "Bei den Universitätsbibliotheken ist die alte unselige Verzettelung der Mittel durch Aufteilung an die Fakultäten oder Fachvertreter beseitigt, bis auf einige wenige Ausnahmen, die in dem Bilde des modernen Bibliothekswesens stark fremdartig anmuten." Milkau, in *Die Kultur der Gegenwart, ihre Entwickelung und ihre Ziele*, p. 569.

49. *Cf.* Andrew D. Osborn, "The Development of Library Resources at Harvard: Problems and Potentialities," in Keyes D. Metcalf, *Report on the Harvard University Library: A Study of Present and Prospective Problems* (Cambridge, Harvard University Library, 1955), p. 93. Also in *HLB*, IX (Spring, 1955), 197–98.

50. John Langdon Sibley, *Letter* [June 7, 1858] *of the Librarian of Harvard College, to the Committee of the Association of the Alumni . . . Appointed to Take into Consideration the State of the College Library* . . . (Cambridge, Metcalf, 1858), pp. 26, 28–29.

51. Harvard University, *Report of the Committee of the Overseers Appointed to Visit the Library* (Boston, 1858), p. 10.

52. *Ibid.*, 1860, pp. 4–5.

53. Justin Winsor, "College and Other Higher Libraries," *LJ*, IV (November, 1879), 400. See also, for the same basic view, Harvard University, *Annual Report of the Librarian, 1894*, p. 17.

54. Charles William Eliot, *Educational Reform: Essays and Addresses* (New York, Century, 1909), p. 229.

55. Columbia University, *Twelfth Annual Report of President Low to the Trustees* (New York, Columbia University, 1901), p. 207.

56. James Hulme Canfield, "The Library: Everybody's Workshop," *Columbia University Quarterly*, VI (June, 1904), 247.

57. Harry Clemons, *The University of Virginia Library, 1825–1950* (Charlottesville, University of Virginia Library, 1954), p. 21.

58. *Ibid.*, p. 98.

59. Letter from Elmer M. Grieder, acting librarian, Stanford, May, 1961.

60. Letter from E. B. Stanford, director of libraries, Minnesota, June, 1961.

61. *Statutes of Cornell University*, May, 1891, Article XIV, pars. 4, 6.

62. Charles A. Kraus, "The Evolution of the American Graduate School," *Bulletin of the American Association of University Professors*, XXXVII (Autumn, 1951), 497–505, especially p. 498.

63. William Warner Bishop, "Resources of American Libraries," *LQ*, VIII (October, 1938), 445–79, especially p. 448.

64. Louis R. Wilson, "The Role of the Library in the Advancement of Scholarship," in *Library Resources of the University of North Carolina*, ed. by Charles E. Rush (Chapel Hill, University of North Carolina Press, 1945), pp. 8–9.

65. Iwinski, *Bulletin de L'Institut International de Bibliographie*, XVI (1911), pp. 6 ff.

III: MODERN SELECTING AND COLLECTING

1. See, for example, University of Chicago, *President's Report, 1927–1928* (Chicago, University of Chicago Press, c.1929), p. 57; Yale University, *Report of the Librarian, 1952–1953* (New Haven, Yale University Press, 1953), p. 6.

2. Fritz Redenbacher, "Die Erwerbung," *Hand.*, II, 224–30; Walter Bauhuis, "Erwerbung, Katalogisierung . . . ," in *Zur Praxis der Wissenschaftlichen Bibliotheken in den USA. (Beiträge zum Buch- und Bibliothekswesen, V)*, ed. by Carl Wehmer (Wiesbaden, Harrassowitz, 1956), pp. 102–6.

3. A briefer account of basic German policy and practice is given in Gisela von Busse, *West German Library Developments Since 1945* (Washington, D.C., Library of Congress, 1962), pp. 27–33, 40–45, 56–57.

4. *Reglement für die Königliche und Universitäts-Bibliothek zu Breslau vom 19. Mai 1815*. Reproduced in *Serapeum*, VI, *Intelligenz-Blatt*, No. 14 (July 31, 1845), 106, 107.

5. *Reglement für die Universitäts-Bibliothek zu Bonn vom 25. August 1819*, Article III, par. 1, Article II, par. 3. Reproduced in *Serapeum*, VI, *Intelligenz-Blatt*, No. 8–11 (1845), 57–61, 65–69, 73–77, 81–85. (Original ms., Bonn, has the title *Reglement für die Bibliothek der Königlich Preussischen Universität zu Bonn*.)

6. *Cf.* Gustav Abb, *Schleiermachers Reglement für die Königliche Bibliothek zu Berlin vom Jahre 1813 und Seine Vorgeschichte* (Berlin, Breslauer, 1926). The work not only gives the history and development

of the *Reglement,* and its text (pp. 88–99), but proves the priority of Schleiermacher's ideas (pp. 39–41).

7. Anton Klette, *Die Selbständigkeit des Bibliothekarischen Berufes, mit Rücksicht auf die Deutschen Universitäts-Bibliotheken* (Leipzig, Teubner, 1871).

8. The first full-time nonprofessor librarians at Leipzig, 1833, and Würzburg (Anton Ruland), 1850, may be considered "sports"; they lacked parallels and began no trend. In the years 1871–1876, however, twelve German universities appointed full-time librarians.

9. "die Aufgabe, eine dauernde Verbindung zwischen dem Lehrkörper . . . und der Verwaltung der Bibliothek herzustellen und auf . . . die zweckmässige Vermehrung der letzteren einen angemessenen Einfluss zu üben." III. *Reglement für die Bibliotheks-Commission der Königlichen Universität zu Göttingen,* Berlin, 8. Februar 1879, p. 2. The Ministerial Decree (*Erlass*) of 27 June 1890 for the University of Berlin contained the same thought and almost precisely the same language (par. 3). Cf. *Chronik der Königlichen Friedrich-Wilhelms-Universität zu Berlin für das Rechnungs-Jahr 1890/91* (Berlin, Becker, 1891), p. 157.

10. "Dass Kommissionen eine Bibliothek wesentlich gefördert haben, dieser Nachweis ist noch nicht erbracht worden." Georg Leyh, "Erlangen UB," *ZfB,* XLIV (June, 1927), 308–9.

11. *Cf.* Arnim Graesel, *Handbuch der Bibliothekslehre,* 2d ed. (Leipzig, Weber, 1902), pp. 334 ff.; and Emil Gratzl, "Die Erwerbung," *Hand.,* 1st ed., (Leipzig, Harrassowitz, 1933), II, 127 ff.

12. An occasional dissenting voice was raised. *Cf.* Gratzl, *Hand.,* 1st ed., II, 129–32. However, even Gratzl's argument was against the system for smaller libraries (p. 132). Most of the scholarly libraries were not "small," or when they were, felt, with considerable justification, that they would not remain so.

13. Ludwig Klaiber, "Das Referatsystem," *ZfB,* LIII (January–February, 1936), 69–73.

14. *Cf.* Georg Leyh, "Die Verwaltungsordnung der Universitätsbibliothek Tübingen vom 17. Juli 1929," *ZfB,* XLVII (January–February, 1930), 29–37. Subject responsibility of the staff is laid down in Pt. II, par. 9, p. 36.

15. Hugo Alker, *Die Universitätsbibliothek Wien: Geschichte, Organisation, Benützung,* 3d rev. ed. (Vienna, the Library, 1957), p. 20. At the time, the library had nineteen *Referenten.*

16. The great national libraries pursue of necessity a parallel policy, or assign selection responsibility by language, or employ a combination of the two. Two of the earliest to institute formal, full-fledged programs were the Royal Library at Berlin and the Court Library at Vienna. See *Jahresbericht der Königlichen Bibliothek zu Berlin, 1905/06,* pp. 8 ff.;

and Friedrich Ritter von Egger-Möllwald, "Das Referatssystem in der Diensteinteilung der k.k. Hofbibliothek in Wien," *ZfB*, XXIX (July–August, 1912), 303–10. For a summary report of contemporary practice, see M.-T. Dougnac, "Les Acquisitions Étrangères dans les Grandes Bibliothèques Scientifiques," *Actes du Conseil de la F.I.A.B.*, 21st Session, Brussels (The Hague, Nijhoff, 1956), pp. 74–75.

17. The basic concept of the *Kaufsitzung* goes back at least as far as 1815. The Breslau statute of that year directs the librarian to meet regularly with his colleagues for the purpose, among others, of arriving at decisions concerning acquisitions. *Reglement für die Königliche und Universitäts-Bibliothek zu Breslau*, par. 6, 7, p. 99.

18. *Jahrbuch der Deutschen Bibliotheken*, XXXVIII, (Wiesbaden, Harrassowitz, 1959), pp. 440–41.

19. This cost figure, and those which follow, obviously include time spent rejecting, as well as selecting books. Figures for number or percent of titles rejected are not generally kept.

20. Walter Bauhuis, *Die Universitätsbibliothek Münster in den Jahren 1957/58 und 1958/59* (Münster, Westfalen, 1959), p. 15. (Photo-reproduced from typescript.) The *Kaufsitzungen* averaged about five hours each and eleven individuals took part. Twelve sessions were held from fall, 1957, to spring, 1958, and twenty-two sessions in the 1958 report year. The total salary cost of the first group was, therefore, about 4,620 DM ($1,155) (11 individuals x 7 DM hourly salary x 5 hours x 12 meetings) and of the second group, 8,470 DM ($2,117) (11 individuals x 7 DM hourly salary x 5 hours x 22 meetings). The first group of meetings bought 658 volumes costing 13,216 DM ($3,304); the second group, 1,856 volumes costing 36,666 DM ($9,166).

21. "Tedious and time-wasting round-table discussions of recommendations for book purchase have long gone by the board, as they should do in all university libraries." George H. Bushnell, "A University Library in Action," *Library Review*, XII (Spring, 1950), 282.

22. See *Gutachten der Sonderkommission des Bibliotheksausschusses der Deutschen Forschungsgemeinschaft über den Personalstand der Niedersächsischen Staats- und Universitätsbibliothek Göttingen*, 1952, p. 5. Mimeograph.

23. "Das Referatsystem ist offenbar nur dann sinnvoll anwendbar, wenn eine ausreichende Anzahl von Bibliothekaren zur Verfügung steht und ihre Wissenschaftsfächer und Interessengebiete eine entsprechende Streuung aufweisen. . . . Ehe das Referatsystem in vollem Umfang und mit aller wünschenswerten Konsequenz durchgeführt werden kann, wird an den meisten deutschen Universitätsbibliotheken . . . vor allem eine beträchtliche Verstärkung des wissenschaftlichen Personals unter Berücksichtigung der verschiedenen Fächer . . . notwendig sein." Reden-

bacher, *Hand.*, II, 232, 234. See also, von Busse, *West German Library Developments Since 1945*, p. 28; Hermann Tiemann, "Das Problem der Universalbibliothek Heute," *NfWB*, VI (1953), 176–77.

24. The word "institute" is used here, and later, generically, as the Germans generally use it, to denote institutes, seminars, clinics, laboratories, and endowed chairs. There is an extensive literature on the subject, mostly in German, covering the history and development, support, and specifically the relation of the institute library to that of the university library. Among the more useful titles are the following: Edgar Breitenbach, "Letter from Germany," *CRL*, XV (October, 1954), 412–16; Karl Bücher, "Universitätsbibliothek und Institutsbibliotheken," in *Hochschulfragen; Vorträge und Aufsätze*, ed. by Karl Bücher (Leipzig, 1912), pp. 145–72; Deutsche Forschungsgemeinschaft, *Instituts- und Hochschulbibliotheken. Denkschrift . . .* (Deutsche Forschungsgemeinschaft, 1955), p. 24; "Erlass, Betreffend die Bibliotheken der Universitäts-Anstalten und deren Beziehungen zu den Universitäts-Bibliotheken" (im Königreich Preussen), *ZfB*, VIII (December, 1891), 550–51; Lennart Grönberg, "Institutions-och Seminariebibliotheken vid Uppsala Universitet . . . ," *Nordisk Tidskrift för Bok-och Biblioteksväsen*, XLVIII (1961), 23–29 (The findings of this investigation of Uppsala University parallel those of the present study and are typical for the Continental university generally.); Karl Julius Hartmann, "Das Problem der Institutsbibliotheken," *ZfB*, LVI (January–February, 1939), 17–37; Ludwig Klaiber, "Um die Einheit der Universitätsbibliothek," *ZfB*, XLVI (January–February, 1929), 28–33; Gottfried Kricker, "Die Zusammenarbeit der Universitäts- und Institutsbibliotheken und der Kölner Versuch ihrer Verwirklichung," *ZfB*, LIV (September–October, 1937), 448–70; Georg Leyh, "Die Universitätsbibliothek im Rahmen der Universität," *ZfB*, L (August–September, 1933), 550 ff.; Georg Leyh, "Stellung und Aufgabe der wissenschaftlichen Bibliothek in der Zeit," *ZfB*, LIII (September–October, 1936), 473–82; Gotthold Naetebus, "Über die Bibliotheken der Preussischen Universitätsinstitute," *ZfB*, XXIII (July–August, 1906), 341–56; Gotthold Naetebus, "Instituts-, Behörden- und andere Fachbibliotheken," *Hand.*, 1st ed., II, 523–65, with extensive references to the earlier literature; Gerhard Reincke, *Gutachten über die Lage der Institutsbibliotheken und ihr Verhältnis zu den Universitäts- und Hochschulbibliotheken* (Deutsche Forschungsgemeinschaft, 1953) (partial English resumé in Breitenbach); Wolf Meinhard von Staa, "Aufbau und Bedeutung der deutschen Universitätsinstitute und Seminare," in *Das Akademische Deutschland* (Leipzig and Berlin, 1930), III, 263–76; Hermann Tiemann, "Das Problem der Universalbibliothek Heute," *NfWB*, VI (1953), 166–77; Tiemann, "Betrachtungen zur Lage und zum Verhältnis der Instituts- und Hochschulbibliotheken," *ZfBB*, III (1956), 4–12; Christoph Weber, "Zusammenarbeit der deutschen Bibliotheken,"

ZfB, XXXVIII (July–August, 1921), 150–63. See also Robert Vosper, "A Recent Look at University Libraries in Italy," *CRL*, XXII (May, 1961), 199–210.

25. "Die Deutschen Universitäts-Bibliotheken, ihre Mittel und ihre Bedürfnisse," in *Sammlung Bibliothekswissenschaftlicher Arbeiten*, ed. by Karl Dziatzko (Leipzig, M. Spirgatis, 1894), No. 6, pp. 40–61.

26. See Reincke, *Gutachten über die Lage der Institutsbibliotheken und ihr Verhältnis zu den Universitäts- und Hochschulbibliotheken*, p. 21; Deutsche Forschungsgemeinschaft, *Instituts- und Hochschulbibliotheken*, p. 12.

27. "Es bekundet sich . . . eine Entwicklung der Institutsbibliotheken zu vollständigen Fachbibliotheken, die nicht mehr neben den Universitätsbibliotheken, sondern über ihnen stehen." Naetebus, *ZfB*, XXIII (1906), p. 357.

28. "das Zeitalter zu Ende geht, in dem die Universitäts-Bibliothek die führende Stellung in der Sammlung und Verwaltung der wissenschaftlichen Literatur für die Universität . . . hatte." Hartmann, *ZfB*, LVI (1939), p. 23.

29. "das Problem [ist] erst heute in einem überreifen Stadium nach seiner ganzen Bedeutung nicht bloss für die wissenschaftliche Arbeit, sondern für die Zentralbibliothek selbst erkannt. Es handelt sich für die Universitätsbibliothek um die Existenzfrage." Georg Leyh, "Die Entwicklungslinie der Göttinger Bibliothek," *ZfB*, LIV (November, 1937), 550.

30. von Busse, *West German Library Developments Since 1945*, pp. 31–32.

31. "wir sind seither in dieser bibliothekarischen Kernfrage keinen Schritt vorwärts, dagegen viele Schritte weiter in das Verhängnis hineingekommen." Hartmann, *ZfB*, LVI (1939), p. 26.

32. Hermann Tiemann, "Grundsätze zur Etatgestaltung bei Hochschul- und Institutsbibliotheken," *ZfBB*, III (1956), 22.

33. "ist es jetzt an der Zeit, wenigstens die Erwerbung [wissenschaftlicher] Produktion durch gleichartige Bibliotheken am gleichen Ort in ein System zu bringen und das Bücherwesen einer Universität als eine Einheit zu behandeln." Leyh, *ZfB*, LIII (1936), 477.

34. "the acquisition policy [of the institute library] may change depending on the personality and scholarly interest of the director." von Busse, *West German Library Developments Since 1945*, p. 33.

35. See Gottfried Zedler, *Geschichte der Universitätsbibliothek zu Marburg von 1527–1887* (Marburg, Elwert, 1896), pp. 121, 135–36.

36. "Erlass, Betreffend die Bibliotheken der Universitäts-Anstalten und deren Beziehungen zu den Universitäts-Bibliotheken," par. 4.

37. *Senat der Freien und Hansestadt Hamburg.* Organisationsamt 121.00–23,8. 21 April 1960 (Memorandum) (CU-Li).

38. "Bei den Formaten der Zettel . . . der Anordnung und dem

Umfang der Titelaufnahmen, der Form und Zahl der Verweisungen u.a.m. sind alle nur möglichen und erdenkbaren Variationen vertreten." Reincke, *Gutachten über die Lage der Institutsbibliotheken und ihr Verhältnis zu den Universitäts- und Hochschulbibliotheken*, p. 24.

39. "Die Fälle, in denen Benutzung im Institut genügt, sind ganz in der Minderheit, und auch dann ist erst eine umständlich einzuholende Erlaubnis des zuständigen Direktors notwendig." Hartmann, *ZfB*, LVI (1939), 21. See also, Kricker, *ZfB*, LIV (1937), 452.

40. "Das Anwachsen und die selbständige Ausbildung der Anstaltsbibliotheken hatte für die Universitätsbibliothek die nachteilige Folge, dass ein Teil der Professoren das frühere oft sehr lebhafte, unmittelbar *persönliche Interesse* an dem Gedeihen der Universitätsbibliothek verlor. Während ehemals alles, was die Universitätsbibliothek an Büchern durch die vorgesetzten Behörden und von Privaten als Geschenk erhielt, selbstverständlich der Universitätsbibliothek zukam, machte sich mehr und mehr ein Wettbewerb der Anstaltsbibliotheken geltend, der oft die Universitätsbibliothek empfindlich schädigte." Wilhelm Erman, *Geschichte der Bonner Universitätsbibliothek* (*Sammlung Bibliothekswissenschaftlicher Arbeiten*, Nos. 37/38) (Halle, Karras, 1919), pp. 272–73. See also, Reincke, *Gutachten über die Lage der Institutsbibliotheken und ihr Verhältnis zu den Universitäts- und Hochschulbibliotheken*, p. 3; von Busse, *West German Library Developments Since 1945*, p. 32.

41. Maurice F. Tauber, C. Donald Cook, and Richard H. Logsdon, *The Columbia University Libraries* (New York, Columbia University Press, 1958), pp. 173, 178.

42. University of Michigan, Institute for Social Research, Survey Research Center, *Faculty Appraisal of a University Library* (Ann Arbor, The University Library, 1961), p. 5.

43. R. E. Buchanan, "The Development and Function of a Research Library, 1922–46," *CRL*, VIII (July, 1947), 295.

44. "viele Gelehrte sich im Laufe der letzten Jahrzehnte so sehr daran gewöhnt haben, sich für ihre Arbeiten ganz auf ihre Institutsbibliotheken zu stützen, dass ihnen deren Ausbau weit dringlicher erscheint als derjenige der zentralen Hochschulbibliotheken, denen sie sich entfremdet haben." Reincke, *Gutachten über die Lage der Institutsbibliotheken und ihr Verhältnis zu den Universitäts- und Hochschulbibliotheken*, p. 3.

45. From conversations with the librarians and *Referenten*.

46. *Merkblatt für die Verwaltung der Instituts- und Seminarbibliotheken in Freiburg i. Br. und Ihre Zusammenarbeit mit der Universitäts-Bibliothek* (Freiburg, 1955), p. 9 (CU-Li). Mimeograph. Among many other documentary evidences may be cited, *Jahresbericht der Universitätsbibliothek Mainz, 1955* (Mainz, 1956), pp. 24–25. Mimeograph.

47. *Jahresbericht der Universitätsbibliothek Kiel, 1959/60* (Kiel, 1960), p. 14.

48. The reference here, of course, is to schools, usually graduate, such as those of architecture, forestry, librarianship, theology, etc.

49. Its course would in all probability also have been different if what is now only a small footnote had turned out otherwise than it did. The classical philologist Wilhelm Studemund became a kind of unofficial library advisor to Friedrich Althoff during much of the period (1882–1907) when that great and effective educator and worker for library improvement was in the Prussian ministry. In 1887 Studemund laid before Althoff a formal memorandum proposing that the seminar and institute libraries be made parts of the university libraries, under the control of the university librarians. Far-sighted and imaginative though Althoff was, he apparently did not see the enormous significance and benefits of the proposal. At any rate, nothing came of it. See Arnold Sachse, *Friedrich Althoff und Sein Werk* (Berlin, Mittler, 1928), p. 285.

50. Harvard University, *Annual Report of the Librarian, 1881* (Cambridge, 1881?), pp. 3–4.

51. George Alan Works, *College and University Library Problems* (Chicago, American Library Association, 1927), p. x.

52. United States Office of Education, *Survey of Land-Grant Colleges and Universities*, 2 vols. (Washington, D.C., Government Printing Office, 1930), I (Office of Education *Bulletin, 1930,* No. 9), 674.

53. American Library Association, *A Survey of Libraries in the United States*, 4 vols. (Chicago, American Library Association, 1926), I, 172.

54. University of California, *Standing Orders of the Board of Regents in Force July 1, 1911*, par. 292, p. 34.

55. Harold L. Leupp, "The Library the Heart of the University," *LJ*, XLIX (July, 1924), 619.

56. *Ibid.*, pp. 620–21.

57. University of California, *By-Laws and Standing Orders of the Board of Regents . . . 1952*, p. 54.

58. University of California, *University Bulletin*, VI (July 29, 1957), 13.

59. Mildred Hawksworth Lowell, "Indiana University Libraries, 1829–1942." Unpublished doctoral dissertation, Graduate Library School, University of Chicago, 1957, p. 272–73, 288.

At Minnesota, in 1924, the Regents adopted resolutions: "That hereafter no separate unit of the University Library be established or maintained outside the general library except with the official approval of the President and the Board of Regents," and "That the University librarian be directed to make provision under his general control and supervision for the various units of the University Library in harmony with the previous recommendation." University of Minnesota Library, *Annual Report for the Year Ending June 30, 1925*, p. 222.

60. Columbia University, *Charters and Statutes with Amendments to*

December 3, 1956 (New York, Columbia University, 1956), p. 18.

61. Northwestern University, "Statement Concerning Library Policies" (Evanston, Ill., 1956) (CU-Li). Mimeograph.

62. For a summary of the earlier history of the departmental library in America, see Lawrence Thompson, "The Historical Background of Departmental and Collegiate Libraries," *LQ*, XII (January, 1942), 49–74; William W. Bishop, "The Problem of the Departmental System in University Libraries," *LJ*, XXVI (January, 1901), 14–18; Henry E. Bliss, "Departmental Libraries in Universities and Colleges," *Educational Review*, XLIII (April, 1912), 387–409; American Library Association, *A Survey of Libraries in the United States*, pp. 168–95; Walter Hausdorfer, "Professional School and Departmental Libraries," *Special Libraries*, XXX (March, 1939), 75–81, XXX (April, 1939), 116–20, XXX (May–June, 1939), 150–56, XXX (July–August, 1939), 191–95; George F. Little, "School and College Libraries," in *United States Bureau of Education, Report of the Commissioner of Education, 1892–1893*, I, Pt. 2, p. 925; Jesse H. Shera, "How Much is a Physicist's Inertia Worth?" *Physics Today*, XIV (August, 1961), 42–43.

63. Institute of International Education, Council on Higher Education in the American Republics, "Inter-American Seminar on University Libraries . . . January 25–27, 1961," p. 3. Mimeograph. Also in *CRL*, XXIII (January, 1962), 28–32.

64. American Library Association, *Survey of Libraries in the United States*, p. 231.

65. United States Office of Education, *Survey of Land-Grant Colleges*, p. 651.

66. *Ibid.*, p. 651.

67. *Ibid.*, p. 652.

68. *Ibid.*, p. 652.

69. E. H. Budington, "Book Selection in the University Library," *Columbia University Quarterly*, XIII (March, 1911), 220–21.

70. Letters from Stanley L. West, director of libraries, Florida, May 21, 1956, and July 8, 1960.

71. Letter from Earle C. Thompson, assistant director for technical services, Louisiana, June 20, 1960; and Louisiana State University Acquisitions Division, "Book Selection Policies and Procedures," May 26, 1953 (CU-Li). Typescript.

72. Letter from Marie Gosebrink, assistant acquisitions librarian, quoting Kenneth S. Allen, acquisitions librarian, Washington (Seattle), June 17, 1960.

73. Letter from Robert A. Miller, director of libraries, Indiana, August 6, 1956.

74. The Johns Hopkins University Library, "Report to the Faculty Library Committee" (February 25, 1955), p. 2 (CU-Li). Typescript.

75. Letter from R. D. Johnson for Elmer Grieder, acting librarian, Stanford, February 14, 1961.

76. Letter from Benjamin E. Powell, librarian, Duke, September 16, 1960.

77. *Reports of the Library Committee and of the University Librarian for the Academic Year 1960–61 to the Berkeley Division, Northern Section of the Academic Senate, University of California*, p. 4.

78. Letter from David Otis Kelley, librarian, New Mexico, November 22, 1955.

79. Cornell University Library, "Proposed Book Fund Allotments, 1961–62," Approved April, 1961. Mimeograph.

80. Memorandum, November 7, 1955, F. Reichmann, assistant director of libraries, to Stephen A. McCarthy, director, Cornell, brought up to date by him, June 16, 1960.

81. Letter from Felix Reichmann, Cornell, November 17, 1961.

82. Letter from Carl Jackson, head of acquisitions department, Minnesota, February 9, 1961.

83. Letter from Herman H. Fussler, director of libraries, Chicago, February 13, 1961.

84. University of Illinois Library, "Acquisition Policy Statement" (Urbana, February, 1959), pp. 1, 3 (CU-Li).

85. Letters from Robert H. Muller, assistant director, Michigan, November 18, 1955, and June 16, 1960; Frederick H. Wagman, director, Michigan, November 14, 1955.

86. University of Michigan Library, "Staff Circular," No. C1, December 7, 1955. Mimeograph. See also, "Staff Circular," No. C16, February 12, 1960 (CU-Li). Mimeograph.

87. "Harvard College Library Acquisitions" (April, 1959), p. 6. Mult. See also, "Subject Collections, Collecting Policies, and Funds," in *Report on the Harvard University Library: A Study of Present and Prospective Problems* (Cambridge, Harvard University Library, 1955), p. 72.

88. Letter from Richard H. Logsdon, director of libraries, Columbia, February 9, 1961.

89. American Library Association, *Survey*, pp. 215–20. See also, Ralph E. Ellsworth, "Summary of Current Practices . . . with Respect to the Management of Book Funds," *CRL*, III (June, 1942), 252–55.

90. Felix Reichmann, "Management and Operation," *Library Trends*, III (April, 1955), 463.

91. *Ibid.*, p. 467.

92. Allocation of funds *to* elements of instruction is, of course, to be distinguished from the presumably necessary administrative device of making rough apportionment *by* broad subject fields.

93. George H. Bushnell, "A University Library in Action," *Library Review*, XII (Spring, 1950), 282. See also, J. W. Scott, "Book Stock:

Building and Maintenance. II. University Libraries," in *Bibliography and Book Stock* (London, Library Association, 1954), pp. 13–14.

94. For discussions of the problem, its variables, and proposed formula, see Donald Coney, "An Experimental Index for Apportioning Departmental Book Funds for a University Library," *LQ*, XII (July, 1942), 422–28, with bibliographical footnote, p. 423; and Ralph E. Ellsworth, "Some Aspects of the Problem of Allocating Book Funds Among Departments in Universities," *LQ*, XII (July, 1942), 486–94, with bibliographical footnote, p. 486. Both authors agree that an ideal, objective solution is not possible. It is perhaps noteworthy that no serious, comprehensive attack on the problem so far as the university library is concerned has been attempted since these two papers.

95. Keyes D. Metcalf, "The Essentials of an Acquisition Program," in *The Acquisition and Cataloging of Books,* ed. by William M. Randall (Chicago, University of Chicago Press, c. 1940), p. 77.

96. *Ibid.,* pp. 77, 78.

97. Robert B. Downs, "Problems in the Acquisition of Research Materials," in *The Acquisition and Cataloging of Books,* p. 75.

98. "Die Vermehrung seiner Bibliothek dem Bibliothekar seine bescheidene, freilich anonyme Unsterblichkeit schenkt." Emil Gratzl, "Die Erwerbung," *Hand.,* 1st ed., II, 129–30.

99. William R. Pullen, "Selective Acquisitions at Yale," in *Studies in Library Administrative Problems,* ed. by Keyes D. Metcalf (New Brunswick, N.J., Rutgers University, Graduate School of Library Service, 1960), pp. 33–34.

100. Keyes D. Metcalf, "Problems of Acquisition Policy in a University Library," *HLB*, IV (Autumn, 1950), 294.

101. *LJ*, XXII (October, 1897), 39–44.

102. See Bauhuis, in *Zur Praxis der Wissenschaftlichen Bibliotheken in den USA*, p. 104.

103. J. Periam Danton, "The Selection of Books for College Libraries: an Examination of Certain Factors Which Affect Excellence of Selection," *LQ*, V (October, 1935), 419–56.

104. University of Illinois Library, "Acquisition Policy Statement" (Urbana, 1959), p. 1. Mimeograph.

105. Letter from Robert A. Miller, director of libraries, Indiana, August 6, 1956.

106. Letter from Robert H. Muller, assistant director, Michigan, November 18, 1955.

107. Letter from Robert H. Muller, Michigan, June 16, 1960.

108. Ernest Cadman Colwell, "Cooperation or Suffocation," *CRL*, X (July, 1949), 196.

109. *Ibid.*

110. Douglas Waples and Harold D. Lasswell, *National Libraries and*

Foreign Scholarship (Chicago, University of Chicago Press, c. 1936), p. 71.

111. *Ibid.*, p. 71.

112. *Ibid.*, pp. 74–75.

113. Edwin E. Williams, "Research Library Acquisitions from Eight Countries," *LQ*, XV (October, 1945), 316.

114. Julian P. Boyd, "A Landmark in the History of Library Cooperation in America," *CRL*, VIII (April, 1947), 109.

115. Williams, *LQ*, XV (1945), 317.

116. Andrew J. Eaton, "Current Political Science Publications in Five Chicago Libraries: A Study of Coverage, Duplication, and Omission," *LQ*, XV (July, 1945), 187–212. Eaton's data showed that the University of Chicago and Northwestern University Libraries held, respectively, only 38.5 and 25.1 percent of 1,338 titles published in 1937. Bibliographical Planning Committee of Philadelphia, *A Faculty Survey of the University of Pennsylvania Libraries* (Philadelphia, University of Pennsylvania Press, 1940); M. Llewellyn Raney, *The University Libraries* (Chicago, University of Chicago Press, c. 1933).

117. Keyes D. Metcalf and Edwin C. Williams, "Book Selection for the Harvard Library," *HLB*, VI (Spring, 1952), 200.

118. Letter from Stanley L. West, director of libraries, Florida, July 8, 1960.

119. Raynard C. Swank, "The Cost of Keeping Books," in *Problems and Prospects of the Research Library*, ed. by Edwin E. Williams (New Brunswick, Scarecrow Press, 1955), p. 47.

120. American Library Association and Association of College and Reference Libraries, College and University Post-War Planning Committee, *College and University Libraries and Librarianship* (Chicago, American Library Association, 1946), p. 36.

121. *Ibid.*, p. 37.

122. Albert Baugh, "Discussion" [to the topic "Comprehensiveness versus Selectivity"], in *Changing Patterns of Scholarship and the Future of Research Libraries* (Philadelphia, University of Pennsylvania Press, 1951), p. 84.

123. Letter from Frederick H. Wagman, director of libraries, Michigan, November 14, 1955.

124. *Cf.* Robert Vosper, "Allocation of the Book Budget: Experience at UCLA," *CRL*, X (July, 1949), 215, 217–18.

125. Ruth Hale, "The Acquisitions Librarian in a University Library," *LJ*, LXIV (October 1, 1939), 735.

126. Letter from Norman L. Kilpatrick, director of libraries, Florida State, May 7, 1957.

127. Felix Reichmann, "Management and Operation," *Library Trends*, III (April, 1955), 467.

128. Herman H. Fussler, "The Larger University Library," *CRL*, XIV (October, 1953), 365.

129. Donald Coney, "The Bases of Selection . . ." in Association of Research Libraries, *Minutes of the Fifty-first Meeting*, 1958, pp. 17–18.

130. Letter from Stephen A. McCarthy, director of libraries, Cornell, November 11, 1955.

131. Letter from John H. Berthel, librarian, Johns Hopkins, June 16, 1960.

132. Letter from Marion A. Milczewski, director of libraries, Washington (Seattle), October 23, 1961.

133. Letters from Ralph E. McCoy, director of libraries, Southern Illinois, January 7, 1957 and June 14, 1960.

134. Letter from Donald Coney, librarian, California, November 29, 1960.

135. Letter from Herman H. Fussler, director of libraries, Chicago, February 13, 1961.

136. Letter from Elmer M. Grieder, acting librarian, Stanford, May 15, 1961.

137. University of Colorado Libraries, *Annual Report for 1960/1961*, p. 1. Mimeograph.

138. University of California, Los Angeles, *Report of the University Librarian to the Chancellor for the Year 1959/60*, p. 2, Mimeograph.

139. Grieder, letter, May 15, 1961.

IV: MODERN BOOK COLLECTIONS

1. M. B. Iwinski, "La Statistique Internationale des Imprimés," *Bulletin de L'Institut International de Bibliographie*, XVI (1911), 6.

2. *American Library Association Bulletin*, XXXV (February, 1941), 104.

3. It is significant that the official *Jahrbuch der Deutschen Bibliotheken* does not even mention the existence of, much less provide any data, on the institute libraries. The *Adressenverzeichnis Deutscher Bibiliotheken* (1950) includes some institute libraries for certain universities, but is most incomplete, and now badly out of date. *Minerva Jahrbuch der Gelehrten Welt*, I, *Europa* (Berlin, de Gruyter, 1952) gives for each German university, a list of its institutes and seminars, but provides no information on their libraries. The data, as of about 1950, of the latest *Minerva* are considerably out of date. *The World of Learning, 1960/1961* and *Europa Year Book, 1961* (London, Europa, 1961) and *Index Generalis, 1954–1955* (Paris, Dunod, 1955) give no information on German university institutes.

4. Max Pauer, *Die Wissenschaftlichen Bibliotheken Münchens. Bestände und Benützung* (Munich, Karl Zink, 1958), pp. 17–39.

5. A post-doctoral scholar, with three years' experience at Yale and two at Göttingen, expressed the judgment that the collection of the mathematics institute at the latter institution was substantially superior to the holdings in mathematics of the Yale University Library.

6. Gifts of books or journals were also received by the German libraries after World War II as a result of efforts by the American Library Association, the America Houses, the Committee for Aid to War-stricken Libraries, the French and British governments, Swiss publishers, the Swedish Association of Librarians, and others.

7. See K. Lelbach, "35 Jahre Bonner Studentenbücherei," *ZfBB*, I (1954), 102–10.

8. "Nach wie vor lehnen es die deutschen wissenschaftlichen Bibliotheken ab, der Unterhaltung zu dienen. Die europäische Universitätsbibliothek fühlt sich für den Bereich des *leisurely reading* im allgemeinen nicht zuständig. Sie besitzt abgesehen davon auch nicht die materiellen Voraussetzungen für eine derartige Einrichtung." Wilhelm Martin Luther, "Die Bibliotheksbenutzung," *Hand.*, II, 362, 433.

9. Granted a gross insufficiency of book funds, the relatively greater lack of nonnative titles is to be expected. The written record in his own language is more useful to more students, and even faculty, than the record in another tongue, and, except for outstandingly important foreign publications, a library may logically be expected first to buy the useful titles of its own country.

10. Peter Scheibert, *Lage und Erfordernisse der Westdeutschen Wissenschaftlichen Bibliotheken. Im Auftrage der Notgemeinschaft der Deutschen Wissenschaft* (Osnabrück, Dietrich, 1951); Deutsche Forschungsgemeinschaft, *Instituts- und Hochschulbibliotheken. Denkschrift der Deutschen Forschungsgemeinschaft* (Bad Godesberg, Deutsche Forschungsgemeinschaft, 1955), pp. 6–7. See also, Hermann Tiemann, "Betrachtungen zur Lage und zum Verhältnis der Instituts- und Hochschulbibliotheken," *ZfBB*, III (1956), 4–12.

11. Scheibert, *Lage und Erfordernisse der Westdeutschen Wissenschaftlichen Bibliotheken*, p. 29.

12. Wilhelm Martin Luther, "Zur Lage der Wissenschaftlichen Bibliotheken," *Deutsche Universitäts Zeitung*, VI (October 12, 1951), 6–9.

13. See, for example, "Marked Rise in Trade Prices Indicated in PW Survey," *Publishers' Weekly*, CLXXX (October 30, 1961), 27; William H. Kurth, "U.S. Book and Periodical Prices—A Preliminary Report," *LJ*, LXXXV (January 1, 1960), 54–57; "Cost of Books Index, 1947–9 to 1958," in *American Library & Book Trade Annual 1961*, ed. by Wyllis E. Wright (New York, Bowker, 1960), p. 85; Frank Vincentz, "Die

Entwicklung der Deutschen Bücherpreise," *Börsenblatt für den Deutschen Buchhandel, Frankfurter Ausgabe,* XIV (March 4, 1958), 253–91; Hermann Tiemann, "Grundsätze zur Etatgestaltung bei Hochschul- und Institutsbibliotheken," *ZfBB,* III (1956), 12–22. Book production in the United States alone increased from 10,000 titles in 1930 to 15,000 titles in 1960; between 1947–1949 and 1960, the prices of American books and periodicals also increased about 50 percent. See United States Office of Education, Library Services Branch, "The Cost of Library Materials: Price Trends of Publication," *Library Statistics,* October, 1961, pp. 4–6, 8.

14. Adalbert Roquette, "Die Deutschen Universitäts-Bibliotheken, ihre Mittel und ihre Bedürfnisse," in *Sammlung Bibliothekswissenschaftlicher Arbeiten* (Leipzig, Spirgatis, 1894), No. 6, pp. 40–61; Roquette, "Die Finanzlage der Deutschen Bibliotheken," in *Sammlung Bibliothekswissenschaftlicher Arbeiten* (Leipzig, Spirgatis, 1902), No. 16, pp. 1–30.

15. *Ibid.,* p. 27, and *ante.*

16. Georg Leyh, "Der Bücheretat der Universitätsbibliothek," *ZfB,* XXXIX (July–August, 1922), 227.

17. *Ibid.,* pp. 231, 234.

18. *Ibid.,* p. 242.

19. Fritz Redenbacher, *Die Universitäts-Bibliothek Erlangen in den Jahren 1948–1958; ein Bericht* (Erlangen, Universitäts-Bibliothek, 1959), pp. 23–24.

20. The formula for computing average yearly rate of growth is as follows, using the figures for Kansas (size in 1960, 874,999 volumes; size in 1920, 136,260 volumes) for illustration: $874,999 \div 136,260 = 6.4215$. Log $6.4215 = .80764$. $.80764 \div 40$ (the length of the period) $= .020191$. Anti-log $.020191 = 104.76$. $4.76\% =$ the average annual rate of growth.

21. United States Office of Education, *Library Statistics of Colleges and Universities, 1959–1960* (Washington, D.C., Government Printing Office, 1961). *Part 1: Institutional Data,* pp. 6–49.

V: WHAT SHOULD BE COLLECTED?

1. "Wie schon der Name der Bibliothek sagt, ist sie in *erster Linie für die wissenschaftlichen Bedürfnisse der Universität* bestimmt . . . Dementsprechend pflegt sie die wissenschaftliche Literatur." Christoph Weber, "Die Universität Kiel," *Der Schleswig-Holsteiner,* X (February, 1929), 74.

2. "Die Bibliothek erwirbt die *wissenschaftlich wichtige* Literatur aller Gebiete . . . ausserdem allgemeinbildendes Schrifttum aller Gebiete, soweit es *wissenschaftlich fundiert* ist." Letter from Hermann Tiemann, librarian, Hamburg, May 13, 1961.

3. Robert L. Talmadge, "The Farmington Plan Survey: An Interim Report," *CRL*, XIX (September, 1958), 379.

4. Samuel C. Bradford, *Documentation* (Washington, D.C., Public Affairs Press, 1950); Arthur M. McAnally, "Characteristics of Materials used in Research in United States History" (Unpublished doctoral dissertation, Graduate Library School, University of Chicago, 1951); P. L. K. Gross and E. M. Gross, "College Libraries and Chemical Education," *Science*, LXVI (1927), 385–89; Rolland E. Stevens, "The Use of Library Materials in Doctoral Research: A Study of the Effect of Differences in Research Method," *LQ*, XXIII (January, 1953), 33–41. See also, B. C. Vickery, "The Use of Scientific Literature," *Library Association Record*, LXIII (August, 1961), 263–68, and References, pp. 268–69; Margaret Egan and Herman H. Henkle, "Ways and Means in Which Research Workers, Executives, and Others Use Information," in *Documentation in Action*, ed. by Jesse H. Shera (New York, Reinhold, 1956), pp. 137–55, and References, pp. 155–59.

5. Stevens, *LQ*, XXIII (1953), 40.

6. *Ibid.*, p. 40.

7. Herman H. Fussler, "Characteristics of the Research Literature used by Chemists and Physicists in the United States," *LQ*, XIX (1949), 19–35, 119–43; Douglas Waples, "Belgian Scholars and their Libraries," *LQ*, X (April, 1940), 231–63.

8. Arthur E. Bestor, Jr., "The Transformation of American Scholarship, 1875–1917," *LQ*, XXIII (July, 1953), 173.

9. Crane Brinton, "Patterns of Research and Changing Library Needs," in *Changing Patterns of Scholarship and the Future of Research Libraries* (Philadelphia, University of Pennsylvania Press, 1951), pp. 10–11.

10. James D. Hart, "What a Scholar Expects of Acquisitions," in *Problems and Prospects of the Research Library*, ed. by Edwin E. Williams (New Brunswick, N.J., Scarecrow Press, 1955), pp. 57–58.

11. William W. Bishop, "The Responsibility of American Libraries for the Acquisition of the Materials of Research," in *The Acquisition and Cataloging of Books*, ed. by William M. Randall (Chicago, University of Chicago Press, c. 1940), pp. 31–32.

12. Maurice F. Tauber, C. Donald Cook, and Richard H. Logsdon, *The Columbia University Libraries. A Report on Present and Future Needs* (New York, Columbia University Press, 1958), pp. 250–51.

13. J. G. de Roulhac Hamilton, "The Importance of Unimportant Documents," *LQ*, XII (July, 1942), 512–14.

14. The original of this article, by Johann Albrecht von Rantzau, appeared under the title, "Individualitätsprinzip, Staatsverherrlichung und Deutsche Geschichtsschreibung," in *Die Sammlung*, V (May, 1950), 284–99. The translation, under the title, "The Glorification of the State in German Historical Writing," in *German History: Some New German*

Views (London, Allen and Unwin, 1954), pp. 157–74. Quoted with the kind permission of the publishers. See also, in the same volume, Walther Hofer, "Toward a Revision of the German Concept of History," pp. 187–205.

15. See Tauber, Cook, Logsdon, *The Columbia University Libraries*, pp. 260–61; John Crerar Library, *Acquisitions Policy. A Review of the Policy Governing the Collections* (Chicago, The Library, 1953), pp. 17–18; Herman H. Fussler, "The Larger University Library," *CRL*, XIV (October, 1953), 366–67; and Keyes D. Metcalf and Edwin E. Williams, "Acquisition Policies of the Harvard Library," *HLB*, VI (Winter, 1952), 18, for somewhat similar breakdowns. Metcalf and Williams suggest (1) " 'Farmington Plan coverage' [as] the most inclusive type of collecting"; (2) " 'Research coverage' . . . to indicate the degree of thoroughness in acquisition necessary to maintain a very strong collection that will meet the ordinary needs of scholars in the field but will not contain a great deal of marginal material"; (3) " 'Reference coverage' . . . a good working collection including the important books on a subject"; and (4) " 'light coverage' . . . a highly selective group of books serving primarily as indications of the varieties of information that are available elsewhere or as sources of information for those working in related subjects." A criticism here is that the Farmington Plan coverage frequently does not equal "all out" collecting; either another step is necessary, or the four given need redefinition in order validly to describe and cover the existing conditions.

16. Keyes D. Metcalf, "The Ever Expanding Demand for Materials and the Threatened Decline of Support . . . ," in *Changing Patterns of Scholarship and the Future of Research Libraries*, p. 34.

17. E. J. James, *Sixteen Years at the University of Illinois* (Urbana, University of Illinois Press, 1920), p. 103.

18. Carl M. White, "The University Library and the Scholar," *Bulletin of the American Association of University Professors*, XXVII (June, 1941), 306.

19. Keyes D. Metcalf, "Problems of Acquisition Policy in a University Library," *HLB*, IV (Autumn, 1950), 293.

20. Boswell, *Life of Johnson*, ed. by G. B. Hill, rev. and enl. by L. F. Powell (Oxford, Clarendon, 1934), II, 344 (6. April 1775).

21. R. E. Buchanan, "The Development and Function of a Research Library, 1922–46," *CRL*, VIII (July, 1947), 294.

22. Ernest H. Wilkins, "The University Library and Scholarship," *HLB*, IV (Winter, 1950), 17.

23. Fremont Rider, *The Scholar and the Future of the Research Library* (New York, Hadham Press, 1944), pp. 79–83.

24. *Ibid.*, pp. 83–84.

25. *Cf.* Herman H. Fussler and Julian L. Simon, *Patterns in the Use*

of Books in Large Research Libraries (Chicago, University of Chicago Library, 1961).

26. "man fühlt sich wie in der Gegenwart eines grossen Capitals, das geräuschlos unberechenbare Zinsen spendet." *Werke,* Weimar edition, Pt. I, XXXV, p. 97.

27. See, for example, Hermann Tiemann, "Das Problem der Universalbibliothek Heute," *NfWB,* VI (1953), 176, for such a proposal and its defense.

28. *Reports of the Library Committee and of the University Librarian for the Academic Year 1960/61 to the Berkeley Division, Northern Section of the Academic Senate, University of California,* pp. 3–4.

29. *Ibid.,* p. 5.

30. Andrew C. Osborn, "The Development of Library Resources at Harvard: Problems and Potentialities" in Keyes D. Metcalf, *Report on the Harvard University Library: A Study of Present and Prospective Problems* (Cambridge, Harvard University Library, 1955), p. 92. Also in *HLB,* IX (Spring, 1955), p. 197.

31. Walter Crosby Eells, "Libraries in the Universities of the World," *CRL,* XV (October, 1954), 434–39.

32. See Robert B. Downs, "Leading American Library Collections," *LQ,* XII (July, 1942), 457–73. "Leading collections" is, of course, a relative phrase; it probably usually implies here great absolute strength, but not necessarily "all-out" or "comprehensive" collection.

33. Louisiana State University, Library Acquisitions Division, "Book Selection Policies and Procedures" (Baton Rouge, 1953), p. 1 (CU-Li). Typescript.

34. University of Illinois Library, "Acquisition Policy Statement" (Urbana, February, 1959) (CU-Li). Mimeograph.

35. Cornell University Library, "Outline of an Acquisition Policy" (Ithaca, 1953, revised to 1960), p. 1 (CU-Li). Mimeograph.

36. An interesting, early expression of this view appears in Section 9 of the Erlangen Rules of 1826 (Chapter II, Note 28).

37. See the report of the commission, created September, 1957, by administrative agreement between the Federal Republic and the eleven States (*Länder*), *Empfehlungen des Wissenschaftsrates zum Ausbau der Wissenschaftlichen Einrichtungen* (Tübingen, Mohr, 1960). Pt. I (*Wissenschaftliche Hochschulen*), pp. 24, 55, 460. In 1913 Germany had a population of 67,000,000, and twenty-one universities and eleven technical institutes, with 79,000 students. West Germany, in 1960, with a population of 55,000,000, had eighteen universities, eight technical institutes and 200,000 students, of whom 138,000 were in the universities.

38. See R. E. Barker, *Books for All* (Paris, UNESCO, 1956), pp. 18–21.

39. Fussler, *CRL,* XIV (1953), 365.

40. "Grundsätzlich sollte eigentlich eine wohl eingerichtete Bibliothek allen Wünschen der Forscher zuvorkommen, so dass die Bücher im Augenblick der Nachfrage schon da sind." Erik Gren, "Zur Frage der Methode der Bücherauswahl in den Wissenschaftlichen Bibliotheken," *Libri*, IX (1959), 73.

41. "Unverantwortliche Lücken wären die Folge, wenn man grundsätzlich abwarten wollte, was von den Benutzern tatsächlich verlangt oder zur Erwerbung vorgeschlagen wird." Fritz Redenbacher, "Die Erwerbung," *Hand.*, II, 176.

42. "die sofortige Nachfrage für die wissenschaftliche Bibliothek kein entscheidendes Kriterium der Erwerbungswürdigkeit eines Buches darstellt; dass also der Bedarf des Tages nicht zur Grundlage für die Auswahl gemacht werden kann." *Ibid.*

43. "Da der Benutzungszweck ein Wesensmerkmal der Bibliothek ist, darf der Benutzungswert nur in Ausnahmefällen ausser acht gelassen werden." *Ibid.*

44. The *Deutsche Forschungsgemeinschaft* supports no *Sondersammelgebiete* (special collecting fields) at the University of Munich, as it does at other German university libraries.

45. See, for example, Roland Baughmann, "The Selection and Acquisition of Rare Books and Related Materials at Columbia University," *Library Resources and Technical Services,* II (Fall, 1958), 271–78; Walter Bauhuis, "Erwerbung, Katalogisierung und Magazinierung in Amerikanischen Wissenschaftlichen Bibliotheken," in *Zur Praxis der Wissenschaftlichen Bibliotheken in den USA,* ed. by Carl Wehmer (Wiesbaden, Harrassowitz, 1956) (*Beiträge zum Buch- und Bibliothekswesen, V*), pp. 85–147, especially, pp. 91–101; Metcalf, *HLB*, IV (1950), 293–303, especially, pp. 295–300; Redenbacher, *Hand.*, II, 152–72, 180–224; James E. Skipper, "The Continuing Program of Book Selection and Acquisition," *Library Resources and Technical Services,* II (Fall, 1958), 265–71; Mortimer Taube, "The Theory of Book Selection," *CRL,* II (June, 1941), 221–25; Maurice F. Tauber, *Technical Services in Libraries* (New York, Columbia University Press, 1954), pp. 41–60; and Louis Round Wilson and Maurice F. Tauber, *The University Library,* 2d ed. (New York, Columbia University Press, 1956), pp. 365–424.

VI: TOWARD AN "IDEAL" BOOK SELECTION POLICY

1. Lawrence S. Thompson, "The Dogma of Book Selection in University Libraries," *CRL,* XXI (November, 1960), 442.

2. In the mid-nineteenth century, the regular book funds at Harvard, Yale, and Columbia amounted to $450, $1,620, and $200 respectively; Columbia averaged 120 added volumes per year. Even this late, Bonn

had only 3,550 talers ($3,195), Erlangen, 3,000 talers ($2,700), Marburg, 2,500 talers ($2,250). Heidelberg was adding 1,500 volumes a year. Around the mid-nineteenth century, world book and journal production may have totaled something like 65,000 and 10,000 titles annually, respectively. The figures are possibly four and twenty times as large today. But university libraries are spending fifty, a hundred, or a thousand times as much for books and journals as they did a century ago. See M. B. Iwinski, "La Statistique Internationale des Imprimés," *Bulletin de L'Institut International de Bibliographie*, XVI (1911), 6, 58; Charles C. Jewett, *Notices of Public Libraries in the United States of America* (Washington, 1851), pp. 33, 71, 120; Julius Petzholdt, *Handbuch Deutscher Bibliotheken* (Halle, H. W. Schmidt, 1853), pp. 49, 121, 197, 258.

3. University of Pennsylvania Library, *Changing Patterns of Scholarship and the Future of Research Libraries* (Philadelphia, University of Pennsylvania Press, 1951), p. 4.

4. See Maurice F. Tauber, *Technical Services in Libraries* (New York, Columbia University Press, 1954), pp. 288–89.

5. Maurice F. Tauber, C. Donald Cook, and Richard H. Logsdon, *The Columbia University Libraries* (New York, Columbia University Press, 1958), p. 83.

6. Lesley M. Heathcote, "Co-operative Book Selection," *LJ*, LXVII (January 1, 1942), 3, 37; Letter from Marion A. Milczewski, director of libraries, Washington (Seattle), October 23, 1961. See also, for past practice at, and a proposal for the future, for Yale, William R. Pullen, "Selective Acquisitions at Yale," in *Studies in Library Administrative Problems*, ed. by Keyes D. Metcalf (New Brunswick, N.J., Rutgers University, Graduate School of Library Service, 1960), pp. 28–29, 36–37.

7. Merton W. Ertell, *Interinstitutional Cooperation in Higher Education* (Albany, N.Y., University of the State of New York, 1957), p. 106.

8. Robert B. Downs, "A Realistic Look at Library Cooperation," in Bibliographical Center for Research, Rocky Mountain Region, *Minutes of the Annual Meeting, 1954,* [Bulletin No. 11] (Denver, Denver Public Library, 1954), pp. 7–8. Mimeograph.

9. Stanley Pargellis, "Building a Research Library," *CRL*, V (March, 1944), 114. The position of the author of this article is, at least in part, at variance with the view expressed above. See also, Mortimer Taube, "Libraries and Research," *CRL*, II (December, 1940), 22–26, 32.

INDEX